Brilliant Bites

75 Amazing Small Bites
for Any Occasion

Maegan Brown

The BakerMama

ROCK
POINT

First published in 2023 by Rock Point, an imprint of The Quarto Group,
142 West 36th Street, 4th Floor, New York, NY 10018, USA
T (212) 779-4972 F (212) 779-6058 www.Quarto.com

Rock Point titles are also available at discount for retail, wholesale, promotional and bulk purchase. For details, contact the Special Sales Manager by email at specialsales@quarto.com or by mail at The Quarto Group, Attn: Special Sales Manager, 100 Cummings Center Suite, 265D, Beverly, MA 01915, USA.

10 9 8 7 6 5 4 3 2 1

ISBN: 978-1-63106-963-5

Library of Congress Control Number: 2023934169

Publisher: Rage Kindelsperger
Creative Director: Laura Drew
Editorial Director: Erin Canning
Managing Editor: Cara Donaldson
Interior Design: Laura Klynstra
Photography: Kelsey Foster
Food Styling: Stephanie Jo Greenwood
Food Styling Assistants: Traci Paga and Amanda Mobley

Printed in China

To Brandon.

Thank you for always supporting me as I pursue my passions and share my creativity with the world! You understand me best and I appreciate your encouragement and advice more than you will ever know. We all thank you for contributing the brilliant savvy sip recipes in this book so everyone can enjoy the delicious cheers that we do. I'm so lucky to get to do life with you and our crew. I love you!

To Baker, Bryce, Barrett, and Brookie.

Thank you for being my proudest cheerleaders. Your pure joy and genuine appreciation are what motivate me. I cherish each and every moment we have together. I'm so grateful to get to raise you with Dada. I love y'all so much!

To Mom and Dad.

I have the utmost appreciation for how you raised me to be confident and chase my dreams. I would not be able to do this if you hadn't challenged me to work hard and encouraged me to be the best I can be at everything I do. I have so much love and respect for you!

To The BakerMama team.

The dream team! What a dream it truly is to get to work with each of you to bring The BakerMama to millions of homes around the world. Your hard work and dedication in what we do and how we share it are incredible. It's never a dull moment and I couldn't do it without you!

To my friends.

Y'all are the best of the best! I'm so fortunate to have such amazing friends who are genuinely excited to support me in all that I do. It means the world to me! I consider you family and I strive to be as fabulous of a friend to each of you as you are to me.

To my followers.

I love sharing with y'all! I'm honored that you welcome me into your homes to help create delicious memories with your loved ones. I wake up every day thankful for your support and eager to inspire you even more. I hope you continue to enjoy it all for years to come!

Contents

Take a Bite!

A MESSAGE FROM MAEGAN

Hi, friends! I'm back again! As I like to say, "Third time's a charmer," and that's exactly what *Brilliant Bites* is. It's been created to charm you with the most brilliantly delicious bites you'll ever eat. I've hopefully been inspiring you already with building *Beautiful Boards* and serving *Spectacular Spreads*, and now I've poured my creativity into *Brilliant Bites*. I promise that you will want to make the bites in this cookbook for years to come. Everything's better when it's bite-size, right?! And I hope these recipes WOW you from the moment you see them to the moment you take that first bite.

My family is obsessed with bite-size foods! They're easy to make, perfectly portioned, simply satisfying, and a savvy way to serve. I'm always thinking of ways to miniaturize our favorite foods because it's such an easy and fun way to eat. The bites I've gathered here are a mix of classic comfort foods and clever concoctions that you'll want to make again and again.

As you'll soon discover, when you serve these bites, everyone will be impressed by them—both by their brilliance and amazing deliciousness. These recipes are fun to serve because everyone will ooh and aah over them and beg for more. For me, there's no greater compliment as a host than to see and hear the enjoyment from everyone as they eat the food I've served them.

They can all be eaten with your fingers or a decorative food pick and are perfect for feeding a crowd or on-the-go enjoyment. I tried to keep these recipes as simple as possible with minimal, easy-to-find ingredients and little effort required. There's just something so satisfying about finger foods—plus there are fewer dishes to clean up. Win-win!

My dream for *Brilliant Bites* is for you to have fun with these recipes every chance you get to make something delicious and memorable for your loved ones.

Enjoy the little things . . . I mean bites!

Maegan

Love at First Bite

What exactly is a bite? Bites (a.k.a. appetizers, finger foods, munchies, tasties, and snackies) are perfectly portioned for party grazing and on-the-go snacking. Every recipe in this book is meant to be enjoyed in one or two bites and eaten with your fingers or a decorative food pick. No utensils or plates are necessary, only a napkin to catch any pesky crumbs. Almost any food can be made bite-size as you'll find out. From breakfast foods, such as eggs Benedict (page 92), and desserts, such as banana splits (page 141), to even cocktails, such as piña coladas (page 182)—the options are endless. These bites may be small, but they're big in satisfaction, and such an easy and impressive way to entertain!

Preparation

All the bites in this cookbook are quick and easy to prepare and don't require any special kitchen tools or unique ingredients because I want anyone and everyone to be able to make and enjoy them! I like to use prepared ingredients, like premade piecrusts and jarred pasta sauce, when bringing most of these bites together, but feel free to use homemade.

Many of these recipes can be prepped ahead of time and then garnished just before serving. Or they can be fully prepared and kept warm in the oven until ready to serve. I keep them warm in an oven-safe pan at 200°F (95°C; gas mark ¼).

My goal when serving my family or hosting a crowd is to have everything as prepared as possible, so when we're ready to eat, I can easily garnish the bites, if necessary, or set them out to start enjoying them. I encourage you to prepare these bites ahead of time so that you can serve them with ease when your crowd is hungry and eagerly awaiting what you've made for them.

All the bites in this cookbook are fun to make, so I also encourage you to get your family, kids, and friends involved for an even more memorable experience. These bites are sure to be remembered either way, but if you have the joy of making them together, they will be even more special. Trust me, you'll want to make them again and again!

Serving

The great thing about bites is that you can serve a selection of them together as the main event or as appetizers before a meal. Artfully arranging them on a platter or board is a perfect way to serve them. They're meant to be set out on the table so everyone can leisurely graze. I like to have themed cocktail napkins and/or appetizer plates alongside the bites. Like I said, they're meant to be eaten with your fingers or a decorative food pick. Maybe Mom was wrong? It is okay to eat with your hands!

If a bite is best enjoyed warm, I'll put some out for everyone to start enjoying and keep the rest warm in a 200°F (95°C; gas mark ¼) oven and replenish the platter as necessary. The same goes for bites to be enjoyed cold or frozen. I'll set some out to start with and leave the rest in the refrigerator or freezer with easy access to replenish the platter as necessary.

Mix & Match

The beauty of the bites in this book is that many of them complement each other so you can serve several at once to make a small or big spread for any occasion. For example, the Charcuterie Board Cracker Bites (page 21) and the Bow-Tie Antipasto Bites (page 83) are great starters to any cocktail party, along with The Sage Bee (page 173) to sip on. Or you could serve the Mini Manicotti Bites (page 45), Chicken Parmesan Meatballs (page 50) and Chopped Kale Caesar Salad Cups (page 34) as a very impressive meal with the Chocolate Chip Cookie Cannoli Bites (page 143) for dessert. If you're hosting a brunch, any sweet and savory combination of the Breakfast Bites (page 89) would satisfy the morning munchies. My hope is that you get creative with how you serve these bites for everyone to enjoy and remember!

Transporting

These bites are so great to take to a party or potluck! They're easy to place on a platter and take anywhere. If they need to be refrigerated until serving, you can arrange them on a platter, cover tightly with plastic wrap, and keep in the refrigerator until ready to transport. If they need to be served warm, I would recommend arranging them in an oven-safe serving dish, covering with foil, and keeping them warm in a 200°F (95°C; gas mark ¼) oven until you're ready to take them to the get-together. Transporting them in an insulated food carrier would help keep them warm in transit, or you could warm them in an oven once you get to your destination. There's only one bite recipe and a few sip recipes in this cookbook that need to be kept frozen, so they would be tricky to transport unless you're just going to the neighbor's or a block party.

Leftovers

What leftovers?! Ha ha! I bet you won't have to worry about leftovers with any of these bites, but if you do, they can certainly be stored to enjoy the next day or even frozen for a later time. It depends on each bite as to how long it will keep and how it's best stored for later enjoyment, so please reference each recipe for quick tips on storing them and how they are best served.

Quantities

Nobody is going to want just one, especially with the bites in this book! They'll be begging for more. The number of bites to make depends on the size of the bite, the occasion, and what else you will be serving. If the bites are meant to be an appetizer or light snack, I usually plan for two or three per person. If the bites are being served as the main event, I plan for two to four per person, depending on the size of the bite and how many other bites are being served. For desserts, I always plan for two per person. You'll quickly learn that everyone will love these bites, and you'll want to make as many as possible.

Bite Essentials

Here are some common kitchen tools and serving supplies you will find mentioned throughout the recipes in this book. It doesn't take much to get started making these tasty bites, and I bet you already own most of these items. And if you don't, you can easily order them online or find them locally. When shopping for food picks, cocktail napkins, and appetizer plates, have fun leaning into the theme of the event; there are lots of incredible options available.

Kitchen Tools

2 large baking sheets

24-cup mini muffin pan

12-cup standard muffin pan

Cookie scoops (1 and 2 tablespoon)

Round biscuit or cookie cutters (1 inch, or 2.5 cm; 1½ to 2 inches, or 4 to 5 cm; 2½ inches, or 6 cm; 3 inches, or 7.5 cm)

Cocktail shaker

Muddler (optional)

Toothpicks

Kitchen-only scissors

Kitchen-only ruler

Airtight storage containers

Pastry bags and decorating tips (optional)

Serving Supplies

Platters and boards

Small bowls (for sauces and dips)

Cocktail glasses

Serving utensils

Honey dipper

Decorative food picks and/or skewers

Cocktail napkins

Appetizer plates

Party Bites

Let's get the party started right with these brilliant bites that are stylish and scrumptious. From bite-size Charcuterie Board Crackers that are just as fabulous to eat as they are to look at and Mini Manicotti that will have everyone oohing and aahing over their adorable deliciousness to Chopped Kale Caesar Salad in baked Parmesan cups for a witty way to serve salad as a starter, all these appetizing bites are guaranteed to be party perfect!

Charcuterie Board Cracker Bites

We all know I love serving charcuterie boards! Charcuterie is the queen of any party, and you can test out that theory with these bites that are easy to grab and graze on. Comprised of my go-to meat and cheese must-haves, all in a bite or two, these will surely satisfy those charcuterie board cravings.

---

24 large round and rectangle entertaining crackers

¼ cup (60 g) fig jam spread

1 round (8 ounces, or 227 g) double-cream Brie, sliced into 24 small wedges

1 block (7 ounces, or 198 g) aged white Cheddar, crumbled into small chunks

12 thin slices soppressata, cut in half and rolled up tightly

6 thick slices hard salami, cut into quarters

6 dried apricots, cut into quarters

24 Marcona almonds

24 whole glazed pecans

12 cornichons

6 pitted kalamata olives, cut in half

24 small sprigs fresh rosemary, for garnishing

Honey with dipper, for drizzling

1. Spread each cracker with ½ teaspoon of the fig jam.

2. Arrange a Brie wedge and some crumbled Cheddar on each cracker.

3. Place a soppressata roll-up and a quarter of hard salami on each cracker.

4. Fill in each cracker with an apricot quarter, Marcona almond, glazed pecan, and a cornichon or olive half.

5. Garnish each cracker bite with a little sprig of rosemary.

6. Serve with honey for drizzling.

Note

These bites can be prepped up to 2 hours in advance. Cover loosely with plastic wrap and store in the refrigerator.

Cacio e Pepe Bites

The party people have spoken, and they want pasta bites! Is there anything more perfect than the combination of the three Ps: pasta, Pecorino, and pepper? The simplicity of these bites is what makes them so special and delicious.

8 ounces (225 g) bucatini or any long pasta, broken into quarters

Nonstick cooking spray, for greasing

2 tablespoons unsalted butter

½ cup (125 g) whole-milk ricotta

1 cup (100 g) finely shredded Pecorino

4 teaspoons ground black pepper, divided

¼ cup (25 g) grated Pecorino or Parmesan

1. In a large pot, cook the pasta to al dente according to the package directions. Reserve 1 cup (240 ml) of the pasta cooking water, then drain the cooked pasta and return it to the pot over medium heat.

2. Preheat the oven to 350°F (180°C; gas mark 4). Spray a 24-cup mini muffin pan with cooking spray.

3. Add the butter to the pasta and stir until melted. Add the ricotta and the shredded Pecorino and stir until melted. Add ½ cup (120 ml) of the reserved pasta water and stir until the sauce is creamy and thickly coating the pasta. If the sauce is not creamy enough, add additional pasta water, 1 tablespoon at a time, until it reaches the desired consistency. Stir in 2 teaspoons of the pepper.

4. In a small bowl, whisk together the grated Pecorino and the remaining 2 teaspoons pepper.

5. Add ¼ teaspoon of the grated cheese mixture to each prepared muffin cup. Shake the pan a bit to spread it out within each cup. Completely fill each muffin cup with the pasta mixture. Sprinkle the top of each pasta cup with ¼ teaspoon of the remaining grated cheese mixture.

6. Bake for 18 to 20 minutes, until the pasta starts to crisp on top and around the edges. Let the bites set in the pan for 5 minutes before removing and serving.

Note

These bites can be prepped a day in advance through step 5 to the point of baking them. Tightly cover with plastic wrap to seal in the moisture and refrigerate, then proceed with step 6.

Steak Frites Bites

Talk about the perfect bite! Steak and fries are a classic combo, so why wait for the main course to enjoy them? Tender, juicy strips of flank steak are wrapped around crispy seasoned fries and served with steak sauce for dipping—everything you want in a bite-size starter.

Frites

1 bag (2 pounds, or 907 g) frozen french fries

1 tablespoon kosher salt

1 tablespoon paprika

1 tablespoon garlic powder

2 teaspoons chili powder

1 teaspoon onion powder

1 teaspoon ground black pepper

1 teaspoon granulated sugar

2 tablespoons olive oil

Steak

1 pound (454 g) flank steak

Kosher salt and ground black pepper, to taste

1 tablespoon olive oil, plus more as needed

Steak sauce, for serving

Supplies

24 decorative food picks

1. **To make the frites:** Preheat the oven according to the package directions of the frozen french fries.

2. In a small bowl, whisk together the salt, paprika, garlic powder, chili powder, onion powder, pepper, and sugar until well combined. Place the frozen fries on one or two large baking sheets and drizzle with the 2 tablespoons olive oil. Toss the fries to coat them evenly in the olive oil, then sprinkle the seasoning mixture over the fries and toss until they are evenly coated.

3. Bake the fries according to the package directions, or until they start to turn golden brown and crisp. Keep warm in a 200°F (95°C; gas mark ¼) oven until you are ready to assemble the bites.

4. **Meanwhile, make the steak:** Slice the steak against the grain into twenty-four ¼-inch-thick (6 mm) strips that are 6 inches (15 cm) long and ¾ inch (2 cm) wide when laid flat. Lay the steak strips flat on the cutting board and season both sides generously with salt and pepper.

5. In a large skillet, heat the 1 tablespoon olive oil over medium-high heat. Cooking in batches, add the steak slices and sear for about 1 minute on each side until slightly charred, adding more oil to the pan as needed. Transfer to a clean work surface.

6. **To assemble:** Wrap a strip of steak around 3 french fries and secure with a food pick. Repeat with the remaining steak strips and fries.

7. Serve with steak sauce for dipping, or place the assembled bites on the same pan the fries were baked on and return to a 200°F (95°C; gas mark ¼) oven to keep warm until ready to serve.

Sushi Taco Bites

MAKES
24
BITES

These bites are a fantastic fusion of two of my favorite foods: sushi and tacos! The satisfying crunch of the sticky rice taco shell filled with spicy fresh salmon is a sushi lover's dream come true and a must-try.

Sushi Rice

3 cups (570 g) cooked sticky rice (you can also find precooked sticky rice in the freezer section at the grocery store)

2 tablespoons rice vinegar

1 tablespoon granulated sugar

1 teaspoon kosher salt

Sesame or canola oil, for coating and cooking

Spicy Salmon Mixture

1 fillet (8 ounces, or 227 g) sashimi-grade salmon, cut into small cubes

2 tablespoons mayonnaise

2 teaspoons sriracha

2 teaspoons fresh lime juice

1 teaspoon soy sauce

Fillings and Garnishes

24 thin slices avocado

1 teaspoon white sesame seeds

1 teaspoon black sesame seeds

Sriracha, for drizzling (optional)

24 thin slices jalapeño

For Serving

Wasabi

Sushi ginger

Soy sauce

1. **To make the sushi rice:** Add the cooked sticky rice to a large bowl. In a small microwave-safe bowl, whisk together the vinegar, sugar, and salt. Microwave for 45 seconds, then whisk again until the sugar and salt are dissolved. Drizzle the vinegar mixture over the rice and stir to combine well. Let the rice cool completely.

2. Coat your hands with oil so that it is easier to handle the rice. Form the rice into twenty-four 1 tablespoon–size balls and place them 3 inches (7.5 cm) apart on a piece of parchment paper. Place another piece of parchment paper on top of the rice balls and flatten each ball to about 3 inches (7.5 cm) in diameter. Use a 3-inch (7.5 cm) round biscuit or cookie cutter to trim each rice disc into a perfectly round patty. (The rice should be tightly packed into a flat circle.)

3. In a large skillet, heat 1 tablespoon of oil at a time over medium-high heat, adding 5 or 6 rice patties at a time to the skillet. Let cook on one side until the patties are toasted and golden brown, 6 to 8 minutes, only searing the one side.

4. Place a 24-cup mini muffin pan upside down near the skillet. Remove the seared rice patties from the skillet and carefully fold each one into a taco shape, with the seared side out, and place in between two muffin cups, pressing down slightly in the center so that the bottom sits flat and can be filled while standing once cooled. Let the rice taco shells set until cooled, about 10 minutes.

5. **Meanwhile, make the spicy salmon mixture:** To a medium bowl, add all the salmon mixture ingredients and mix until well combined. Cover and refrigerate until ready to use.

6. **To assemble:** Fill each rice taco shell with an avocado slice and some salmon mixture. Sprinkle with a pinch each of white and black sesame seeds, drizzle with sriracha (if using), and top with a jalapeño slice.

7. Serve with wasabi, sushi ginger, and soy sauce.

Enchilada Egg Rolls

These bites are so fun and yummy that I bet you can't eat only one! The simplicity of the ingredients is what brings such big flavor to a small bite—classic enchilada filling wrapped in a crunchy wonton wrapper, dipped in enchilada sauce, and topped with extra cheese.

1 cup (195 g) shredded rotisserie chicken, skin removed

1½ cups (360 ml) enchilada sauce, divided

1 cup (112 g) shredded Mexican-style cheese blend, divided

½ teaspoon kosher salt

48 wonton wrappers

Chopped green onions, for garnishing

Sour cream, for serving

1. Preheat the oven to 375°F (190°C; gas mark 5). Line two baking sheets with parchment paper (or bake in batches).

2. In a medium bowl, stir together the shredded chicken, ½ cup (120 ml) of the enchilada sauce, ½ cup (56 g) of the shredded cheese, and the salt.

3. Place another ½ cup (120 ml) of the enchilada sauce in a small serving bowl and set aside to serve with the bites for dipping.

4. Put the remaining ½ cup (120 ml) enchilada sauce in a separate small bowl. Working with one wonton wrapper at a time, brush both sides of the wrapper with this enchilada sauce. Lay the wonton wrapper flat and place 1 teaspoon of the chicken mixture down the center of the wrapper. Wrap each one up like a little burrito by first folding in the sides, then folding up the bottom and tightly rolling upward. Fold one side over the filling, tuck the sides in, then fold the other side over to seal it all together. Repeat with the remaining wonton wrappers and filling.

5. Dip each wrapped bite in the remaining enchilada sauce to coat it completely and place, seam side down, on the prepared baking sheet. Sprinkle each enchilada with a little of the remaining cheese.

6. Bake on the middle rack of the oven for 18 to 20 minutes, until the edges and cheese are golden brown.

7. Garnish with green onions and serve with sour cream and the reserved enchilada sauce for dipping.

Note

These bites can be made up to 2 days in advance. Store in an airtight container in the refrigerator, then reheat in the oven at 350°F (180°C; gas mark 4) for about 5 minutes, or until crisp and heated through. Garnish with the chopped green onions before serving.

Blooming Onion Bites

These mini masterpieces will be the talk of any party because they're too tasty to be true! Crispy, slightly sweet, and seasoned just right, these baked bites are served with that classic sauce everyone loves on the side. They will take a bit of patience to prepare, but they're worth the extra effort.

Blooming Onion Bites

Nonstick cooking spray, for greasing

24 white pearl onions (about 1½ inches, or 4 cm, in diameter)

2 large eggs

½ cup (25 g) plain bread crumbs

¼ cup (30 g) all-purpose flour

1 tablespoon granulated sugar

1 teaspoon garlic powder

1 teaspoon onion powder

1 teaspoon paprika

½ teaspoon kosher salt

¼ teaspoon ground black pepper

Dipping Sauce

½ cup (110 g) mayonnaise

2 tablespoons ketchup

2 teaspoons horseradish

½ teaspoon paprika

½ teaspoon garlic powder

¼ teaspoon dried oregano

¼ teaspoon kosher salt

Pinch of ground black pepper

Pinch of cayenne pepper

1. **To make the blooming onion bites:** Preheat the oven to 400°F (200°C; gas mark 6). Line a baking sheet with foil and spray with nonstick cooking spray.

2. Cut the pearl onions into blooms by removing the pointy end of each onion, then peel away the outer skin. Do not cut off the base because that will hold it together. Lay an onion cut side down and, starting ⅛ inch (3 mm) from the top, make vertical cuts downward all around the onion. You should have 5 or 6 slits, depending on the size of the onion. The intact base will hold the onion pieces together. Separate the layers with your hands so they start to bloom out. Repeat with the remaining onions.

3. In a medium bowl, whisk together the eggs and 1 tablespoon of water until well combined, then transfer to a large resealable plastic bag. Add the onions to the bag and toss to coat in the egg mixture.

4. In a separate medium bowl, stir together the bread crumbs, flour, sugar, 1 teaspoon garlic powder, onion powder, 1 teaspoon paprika, ½ teaspoon salt, and ¼ teaspoon black pepper for the coating. Pour the mixture into another large resealable plastic bag. Transfer the onions to the bag, seal, and toss until the onions are coated completely.

5. Place the onions on the prepared baking sheet, bloom sides up, and spray them with cooking spray. Bake on the middle rack of the oven for 20 minutes, or until golden brown and crisped all over. If they are not crispy enough, turn the broiler on high and broil them for a few minutes, watching them carefully so that they do not burn. Let set for a few minutes on the pan before serving.

6. **Meanwhile, make the dipping sauce:** In a small bowl, whisk together all the sauce ingredients until well combined.

7. Serve with the dipping sauce, or keep warm in a 200°F (95°C; gas mark ¼) oven until ready to serve so that they stay crisp.

Meatball Lasagna Cups

MAKES
12
BITES

These lasagna cups make for an amazing appetizer or just a fun way to serve lasagna for dinner! Classic lasagna ingredients—tomato sauce, three cheeses, meatballs, and lasagna noodles—come together in a fun, tasty, and convenient little package.

9 wavy lasagna noodles

2 tablespoons olive oil

Nonstick cooking spray, for greasing

¼ cup (25 g) shredded Parmesan

1 cup (245 g) whole-milk ricotta

2 tablespoons finely grated Parmesan, plus more for garnishing

¼ teaspoon kosher salt

Pinch of ground black pepper

¼ cup (60 ml) pizza sauce

¾ cup (85 g) shredded mozzarella

24 mini frozen baked meatballs (or 6 regular frozen baked meatballs, slightly defrosted and cut into quarters)

2 tablespoons chiffonade-cut or chopped fresh basil, for garnishing (optional)

Note

These bites can be prepped a day in advance through step 5 to the point of baking. Store in an airtight container in the refrigerator, then bake, garnish, and serve per steps 6 and 7.

1. Cook the lasagna noodles to al dente according to the package directions. Drain and lay the noodles in a single layer on a baking sheet to cool. Working with one cooked lasagna noodle at a time, brush all over with the olive oil to keep the pasta from drying out.

2. Preheat the oven to 375°F (190°C; gas mark 5). Line 12 cups of a mini muffin pan with baking cups and spray with nonstick cooking spray.

3. To make the bottoms of the lasagna bites, use a 2-inch (5 cm) round biscuit or cookie cutter to cut 4 circles each from 3 of the lasagna noodles until you have 12 lasagna rounds. Place a round in the bottom of each lined muffin cup. Sprinkle the top of each lasagna round with 1 teaspoon of the shredded Parmesan.

4. Slice each of the remaining 6 lasagna noodles lengthwise into 3 equal-size strips that measure about ¾ inch (2 cm) wide. Discard the middle strip or use it for something else; you only want to use the wavy strips. Cut each of the wavy strips in half crosswise so that you have 12 strips measuring about 6 x ¾ inch (15 x 2 cm). Take one strip at a time and form it into a circle so that the ends just meet. Place the circle, wavy side up, into a muffin cup on top of the shredded Parmesan so that it creates a circle to fill.

5. In a small bowl, stir together the ricotta, grated Parmesan, salt, and pepper. Scoop 1 tablespoon of the ricotta mixture into each of the lasagna noodle cups, then scoop 1 teaspoon of pizza sauce on top and finish each with 1 tablespoon mozzarella and 2 mini meatballs. Spray or brush around the edges of each lasagna cup with some cooking spray.

6. Bake on the middle rack of the oven for about 25 minutes, or until the cheese melts and starts to turn golden brown on top.

7. Let the lasagna cups set in the pan for 10 minutes before serving. Garnish with more grated Parmesan and sliced basil (if using).

Chopped Kale Caesar Salad, Cups

Salad as a finger food?! These Caesar salad cups will exceed your expectations with how easy they are to make and how irresistible they are to eat. The crispy Parmesan cups elevate the experience, complementing the fresh crunch of the kale.

Baked Parmesan Cups

1½ cups (150 g) shredded Parmesan (do not use finely grated cheese)

Caesar Dressing

½ cup (120 ml) mayonnaise

1 tablespoon extra-virgin olive oil

1 tablespoon fresh lemon juice

1 tablespoon grated Parmesan

1 small clove garlic, minced

1 tablespoon Dijon mustard

½ teaspoon Worcestershire sauce

¼ teaspoon kosher salt

Pinch of ground black pepper

Salad

4 cups (260 g) packed finely chopped kale

⅓ cup (32 g) crushed croutons, plus 2 tablespoons for garnishing

⅓ cup (30 g) shredded Parmesan, plus ¼ cup (25 g) for garnishing

1. **To make the Parmesan cups:** Preheat the oven to 375°F (190°C; gas mark 5). Line two baking sheets with parchment paper (or bake in batches).

2. Spread out 1 tablespoon of the shredded Parmesan on the prepared baking sheet to about 3 inches (7.5 cm) in diameter. Repeat with the cheese to make 24 bowls, spacing the Parmesan rounds a few inches (7.5 cm) apart to give them room to spread as they bake. Bake for 4 to 5 minutes, until golden brown all over. Let cool for 30 seconds.

3. Turn a 24-cup mini muffin pan upside down. Using a spatula, carefully lift the Parmesan rounds off the baking sheet, then firmly press each one over the bottom of a separate muffin cup so that the cheese stays in place and takes the shape of a cup as it cools completely. Carefully remove the cups from the pan.

4. **To make the Caesar dressing:** In a large bowl, whisk together the mayonnaise, oil, lemon juice, grated Parmesan, garlic, Dijon, Worcestershire, salt, and pepper until well combined.

5. **To make the salad:** Add the chopped kale to the bowl with the dressing and toss to coat well. Stir in the ⅓ cup (32 g) crushed croutons and ⅓ cup (30 g) shredded Parmesan.

6. Fill each Parmesan cup with 2 tablespoons of the salad, then garnish with a sprinkle of shredded Parmesan and crushed croutons.

Notes

- The Parmesan cups can be made up to 5 days in advance. Store in an airtight container in the refrigerator.

- The salad cups can be prepped a few hours in advance with the salad in them. Cover with plastic wrap and refrigerate until ready to serve, then garnish with the Parmesan and croutons.

Chicken Fajita Bites

MAKES

24

BITES

Skip the tortillas and stuff mini peppers with all the great flavor of sizzling chicken fajitas for a finger food that's sure to be a fiesta favorite!

Chicken Fajita Bites

Nonstick cooking spray, for greasing

6 red mini sweet peppers, 4 whole and 2 finely chopped, divided

6 yellow mini sweet peppers, 4 whole and 2 finely chopped, divided

6 orange mini sweet peppers, 4 whole and 2 finely chopped, divided

2 tablespoons olive oil

¼ medium onion, finely chopped

1 teaspoon paprika

1 teaspoon chili powder

1 teaspoon ground cumin

1 teaspoon kosher salt

4 boneless, skinless chicken tenders (about ½ pound, or 227 g), finely chopped

2 tablespoons fresh lime juice

1 cup (112 g) shredded Mexican-style cheese blend

Chopped fresh cilantro, for garnishing

Key lime wedges, for serving (optional)

Sour Cream Avocado Sauce

¼ cup (55 g) well-mashed avocado (about ½ avocado)

¼ cup (60 ml) sour cream

1 tablespoon fresh lime juice

½ teaspoon kosher salt, or to taste

1. **To make the chicken fajita bites:** Preheat the oven to 400°F (200°C; gas mark 6). Line a 13 x 9-inch (33 x 23 cm) baking sheet with foil and spray with nonstick cooking spray.

2. Slice each whole mini pepper in half lengthwise, leaving the stem intact, and remove any seeds and pith. Slice a small sliver off the back of each half so that it sits flat on the baking sheet, being careful not to slice all the way through. Arrange the peppers in a single layer, cut sides up, on the prepared baking sheet.

3. Heat the oil in a large skillet over medium-high heat. Add the chopped peppers and onion and cook and stir until just tender, about 4 minutes. Transfer to a bowl.

4. In a small bowl, whisk together the paprika, chili powder, cumin, and 1 teaspoon salt until well combined. Add the chopped chicken to a large bowl and toss it with the 2 tablespoons lime juice, then add the seasoning mixture to the bowl and thoroughly coat the chicken.

5. Add the chicken to the same skillet the peppers and onion were cooked in and cook over medium-high heat, stirring occasionally, until the chicken is cooked all the way through, about 4 minutes. Return the peppers and onion to the skillet and toss to combine with the chicken. Remove from the heat.

6. Completely fill each mini pepper half with the chicken fajita mixture, then top with a little shredded cheese. Bake for 13 to 15 minutes, until the cheese melts and the peppers are soft.

7. **Meanwhile, make the sour cream avocado sauce:** In a medium bowl, whisk together all the sauce ingredients until well combined.

8. Drizzle some of the sauce onto each bite, garnish with a sprinkle of fresh cilantro, and serve with lime wedges (if using) for squeezing.

Note

These bites can be prepped a day in advance to the point of baking. Store in an airtight container in the refrigerator, then bake per step 6, though they will need a few more minutes in the oven.

Pad Thai Cups

Forgo Thai takeout with these tasty bites! Everyone loves pad thai, and these simple bites pack all the flavor of the real deal.

Wonton Cups and Noodles

Nonstick cooking spray, for greasing

2 teaspoons sesame oil, divided

24 square wonton wrappers

4 ounces (115 g) pad thai rice noodles

Sauce

2 tablespoons brown sugar

1 tablespoon soy sauce

1 tablespoon fish sauce

1 tablespoon fresh lime juice

2 teaspoons sriracha sauce

Filling

2 tablespoons sesame oil

2 cloves garlic, minced

2 green onions, thinly sliced

½ cup (45 g) finely chopped red bell pepper

½ cup (45 g) chopped bean sprouts

½ cup (55 g) shredded carrot

1 large egg, lightly beaten

4 ounces (113 g) frozen cooked salad shrimp

2 tablespoons chopped peanuts

2 tablespoons chopped fresh cilantro

Pinch of crushed red pepper flakes

Garnishes

Chopped peanuts

Chopped fresh cilantro

Crushed red pepper flakes (optional)

Fresh lime wedges, for serving

1. **To make the wonton cups and noodles:** Preheat the oven to 375°F (190°C; gas mark 5). Grease a 24-cup mini muffin pan with nonstick cooking spray. Using 1 teaspoon of the sesame oil, lightly brush both sides of the wonton wrappers, then carefully press each one into a prepared muffin cup. Bake for 4 to 5 minutes, until crispy and golden brown all over. Leave in the pan until ready to fill and serve.

2. Bring a small pot of water to a boil. Meanwhile, break the noodles into small pieces. Remove the pot from the heat, add the broken noodles, and let soak for 6 to 8 minutes, stirring a few times to separate them, until the noodles are soft but still slightly firm and chewy. Drain and transfer to a bowl. Toss the noodles with the remaining 1 teaspoon sesame oil.

3. **To make the sauce:** In a small bowl, whisk together all the sauce ingredients until well combined.

4. **To make the filling:** In a large skillet, heat the 2 tablespoons sesame oil over medium-high heat. Add the garlic and cook and stir for 1 minute, or until fragrant. Add the green onions, red bell pepper, bean sprouts, and shredded carrot and cook and stir until tender, about 3 minutes. Move the vegetables to one side of the skillet and add the beaten egg. Scramble the egg, breaking it into small pieces with a spatula as it cooks. Once scrambled, combine it with the vegetables in the skillet. Add the cooked noodles and salad shrimp and stir to toss. Add the sauce and gently toss to combine well. Remove the skillet from the heat and stir in the 2 tablespoons chopped peanuts, 2 tablespoons cilantro, and pinch of red pepper flakes.

5. **To assemble:** Place a heaping tablespoon of filling inside each wonton cup. Garnish with chopped peanuts, cilantro, and red pepper flakes (if desired) and serve with lime wedges for squeezing.

Note

The wonton cups can be made a day in advance. Store in an airtight container at room temperature and enjoy within 24 hours of baking.

Ramen Bites

Enjoy all the comfort of a big bowl of ramen in one deliciously satisfying bite! These bites are fun to serve because they surprise everyone with their charming presentation.

Jammy Soft-Boiled Ramen Eggs

1 tablespoon plus 1 teaspoon rice wine vinegar, divided

10 large eggs

2 cups (500 ml) beef broth

½ cup (120 ml) soy sauce

2 cloves garlic, minced

1 tablespoon dark brown sugar

Ramen

1 package (3 ounces, or 85 g) instant ramen noodles

2 tablespoons sesame oil

2 cloves garlic, minced

1 tablespoon soy sauce

1 teaspoon ground ginger

1 teaspoon dark brown sugar

Garnishes

Sriracha sauce

Kosher salt

Sesame seeds (black and white)

2 green onions, thinly sliced

2 small radishes, thinly sliced

2 small jalapeños, thinly sliced

Note

The ramen noodle nests can be made up to 3 days in advance. Store in an airtight container at room temperature, then reheat in the oven at 350°F (180°C; gas mark 4) for about 5 minutes, or until crisp.

1. **To make the jammy ramen eggs:** Bring a large pot of water to a boil. Add 1 tablespoon of the vinegar and carefully lower each egg into the pot. Cook for 7 minutes for room-temperature eggs or 8 minutes for cold eggs straight from the refrigerator. (Timing is important to get a jammy yolk.) Transfer the eggs to an ice bath to stop cooking. Once cooled, carefully peel them. Place the eggs in a large storage container or resealable plastic bag.

2. In a large bowl, whisk together the beef broth, ½ cup (120 ml) soy sauce, garlic, remaining 1 teaspoon vinegar, and 1 tablespoon brown sugar until well combined. Gently pour the marinade into the container or plastic bag with the eggs and seal. Marinate the eggs in the soy mixture for at least 3 hours, or up to 3 days, in the refrigerator. When ready to serve, slice a thin piece off each end of the eggs, then slice each egg crosswise into 2 or 3 rounds that are about ¼ inch (6 mm) thick.

3. **To make the ramen:** Cook the ramen noodles according to the package directions, but DO NOT use the flavor packet that comes with the noodles. Drain.

4. Preheat the oven to 375°F (190°C; gas mark 5). Line a baking sheet with parchment paper.

5. In a medium pot, heat the sesame oil over medium heat. Add the garlic and cook and stir for 1 minute, or until fragrant, then add the 1 tablespoon soy sauce, ginger, and 1 teaspoon brown sugar. Whisk to combine and bring to a simmer. Add the cooked ramen noodles and toss gently to coat completely in the sauce.

6. Place the ramen noodles in heaping 1 tablespoon nests on the prepared baking sheet. You should get about 20 ramen nests. Bake for 15 to 20 minutes, until the ramen nests are golden brown all over and slightly crunchy around the edges. Let cool on the baking sheet for 10 minutes.

7. **To assemble:** Top each ramen nest with a slice of egg, then drizzle with sriracha and garnish with salt, sesame seeds, and the slices of green onion, radish, and jalapeño.

Taco Salad, Cups

MAKES
24
BITES

Taco about the perfect party bite! This scaled-down version of the normally super-sized taco salad is fresh and fun for everyone. And the scoop-shaped chips are the perfect carrier of salad from plate to mouth.

24 scoop-shaped tortilla chips

2 cups (110 g) shredded romaine lettuce

½ cup (90 g) black beans, drained and rinsed

½ cup (75 g) Mexican-style corn or whole kernel corn, drained

¼ cup (45 g) diced tomato

2 tablespoons ranch dressing

½ cup (56 g) shredded Mexican-style cheese blend, divided

¼ cup (60 ml) sour cream, for garnishing

¼ cup (60 ml) guacamole, for garnishing

Hot sauce, for garnishing (optional)

Salsa, for serving

1. Arrange the chips in a single layer on a large platter or baking sheet.

2. Add the lettuce, black beans, corn, tomato, and ranch dressing to a large bowl. Toss the ingredients until evenly coated in the dressing. Stir in ¼ cup (28 g) of the cheese.

3. To assemble, scoop 1 tablespoon of the salad mixture into each chip and sprinkle with a little of the remaining cheese.

4. Garnish each taco salad cup with a dollop each of sour cream and guacamole and a dash of hot sauce (if using).

5. Serve with salsa for topping or dipping.

Mini Manicotti Bites

These one-bite wonders are sure to satisfy all your pasta cravings! Your guests will be impressed by the look and taste of this clever twist on classic manicotti using large rigatoni noodles.

Mini Manicotti

24 large rigatoni (no. 24)

1 tablespoon olive oil

2 tablespoons thick marinara sauce, for topping

Filling

½ cup (125 g) whole-milk ricotta

¼ cup (30 g) shredded mozzarella

2 tablespoons grated Parmesan

½ teaspoon garlic salt

½ teaspoon dried Italian seasoning

Parmesan Seasoning

1 tablespoon grated Parmesan

1 teaspoon dried Italian seasoning

¼ teaspoon garlic salt

Garnish

¼ cup (25 g) finely shredded Parmesan

Supplies

24 decorative food picks

1. **To make the mini manicotti:** Preheat the oven to 350°F (180°C; gas mark 4). Line a baking sheet with parchment paper.

2. Cook the rigatoni to al dente according to the package directions. Drain and toss with the olive oil.

3. Arrange the cooked rigatoni in a single layer on the prepared baking sheet.

4. **To make the filling:** In a medium bowl, stir together all the filling ingredients until well combined.

5. Place the cheese mixture in a piping bag fitted with a round decorating tip or a resealable plastic bag with a corner snipped off. Fill each cooked pasta shell with the cheese mixture.

6. Top each shell with ¼ teaspoon of the marinara sauce. Bake for 10 minutes, or until the filling is bubbling.

7. **Meanwhile, make the Parmesan seasoning:** In a small bowl, whisk together all the seasoning ingredients until well combined.

8. Remove the mini manicotti from the oven and garnish each one with a sprinkle each of finely shredded Parmesan and the Parmesan seasoning.

9. Serve with the food picks for easy eating.

Note

These bites can be prepared up to 2 days in advance through step 5. Store in an airtight container in the refrigerator, then top with marinara sauce and proceed with steps 6 through 9.

Elote Bites

These bites capture the familiar flavors of classic Mexican street corn! Charred baby corn are slathered with a slightly sweet mixture of mayo, garlic, and lime and topped with lots of queso fresco and fresh cilantro. They're quick to make and cute to serve, and perfect for Taco Tuesday or Cinco de Mayo—alongside a margarita, of course.

1 tablespoon olive oil

24 pickled whole baby corn

½ cup (120 g) mayonnaise

2 cloves garlic, minced

2 teaspoons fresh lime juice

1 teaspoon granulated sugar

Pinch of kosher salt

1 cup (120 g) crumbled queso fresco

Tajín seasoning, for garnishing

2 tablespoons finely chopped fresh cilantro, for garnishing

Hot sauce, for serving

1. Heat the oil in a large grill pan or skillet over medium-high heat.

2. Add the baby corn to the hot pan and cook until charred on all sides, turning occasionally, 5 to 6 minutes.

3. In a small bowl, whisk together the mayonnaise, garlic, lime juice, sugar, and salt until well combined. Brush the baby corn all over with the mayonnaise mixture to coat completely.

4. Place the queso fresco in a shallow bowl, then roll each mayonnaise-coated corn in the crumbled queso fresco until mostly coated.

5. Place the corn on a platter and sprinkle each one with a little Tajín seasoning and chopped fresh cilantro.

6. Serve with hot sauce and the remaining mayonnaise mixture for dipping.

Note

These bites can be made up to 2 days in advance. Store in an airtight container in the refrigerator, then enjoy cold or let come to room temperature. They also can be reheated in an oven at 300°F (150°C; gas mark 2) for 5 to 10 minutes.

'Wedge Salad Bites

MAKES
60
BITES

These sophisticated bites are sure to delight! Your guests will be wowed by the creative use of roasted brussels sprouts as the base that's topped with all the yummy components of a great wedge salad—blue cheese, tomatoes, and bacon.

Wedge Salad Bites

15 large or 30 small brussels sprouts

2 tablespoons olive oil

Kosher salt and ground black pepper, to taste

8 slices bacon, cut into 1-inch (2.5 cm) pieces

⅓ cup (75 ml) chunky blue cheese dressing

30 cherry tomatoes, cut in half

⅓ cup (45 g) crumbled blue cheese

Supplies

60 decorative food picks

1. Preheat the oven to 400°F (200°C; gas mark 6). Line a rimmed baking sheet with foil.

2. Remove the bottoms and outer layers from the brussels sprouts, then cut each into 4 wedges for large ones and 2 wedges for small ones.

3. Spread out the wedges on the prepared baking sheet and generously drizzle with the olive oil and sprinkle with salt and pepper. Toss the sprouts with your hands to ensure they're evenly coated. Arrange in an even layer with the inside of each wedge facing up.

4. Bake in the oven for about 20 minutes, or until tender and just starting to brown on top.

5. Meanwhile, cook the bacon so that it is crispy yet still soft enough to fit easily onto a food pick without breaking. Transfer to a paper towel–lined plate to drain, then cut each slice into 1-inch (2.5 cm) pieces.

6. To assemble, dollop ¼ teaspoon of blue cheese dressing onto each brussels sprout wedge. Place a cherry tomato half and a piece of bacon onto a food pick, sprinkling blue cheese crumbles onto the bacon, then insert the food pick into the top of the sprout wedge. Repeat until you have 60 bites.

Note

The brussels sprouts and bacon can be made a day in advance. Store separately in airtight containers in the refrigerator, then assemble the bites when ready to serve.

Chicken Parmesan Meatballs

This creative twist on a classic Italian dish takes chicken Parm to the next level of deliciousness! Perfect for a party, these meatballs also can be served alongside some pasta and a salad for dinner.

Meatballs

1 pound (454 g) ground chicken

½ cup (22 g) Italian-style bread crumbs

¼ cup (25 g) finely grated Parmesan

1 tablespoon dried Italian seasoning

2 cloves garlic, minced

1 large egg, lightly beaten

½ teaspoon crushed red pepper flakes

½ teaspoon kosher salt

¼ teaspoon ground black pepper

20 mini mozzarella balls (ciliegine)

Nonstick cooking spray, for greasing

Coating

1 cup (125 g) all-purpose flour

3 large eggs

3 tablespoons milk

1 cup (45 g) Italian-style bread crumbs

½ cup (50 g) finely grated Parmesan

1 teaspoon dried Italian seasoning

½ teaspoon crushed red pepper flakes

¼ teaspoon kosher salt

Pinch of ground black pepper

1. Preheat the oven to 375°F (190°C; gas mark 5). Line a 13 x 9-inch (33 x 23 cm) rimmed baking sheet with parchment paper.

2. **To make the meatballs:** In a large bowl, stir together the ground chicken, ½ cup (22 g) bread crumbs, ¼ cup (25 g) Parmesan, 1 tablespoon Italian seasoning, garlic, egg, ½ teaspoon red pepper flakes, ½ teaspoon salt, and ¼ teaspoon black pepper until well combined. Scoop the meatball mixture into twenty 2 tablespoon–size portions. Flatten each meatball and place a mozzarella ball in the center. Re-form into balls around the cheese to completely cover the cheese.

3. **To coat the meatballs:** Fill a shallow bowl with the flour. In a second shallow bowl, whisk together the eggs and milk until pale in color. In a third shallow bowl, stir together the 1 cup (45 g) bread crumbs, ½ cup (50 g) Parmesan, 1 teaspoon Italian seasoning, ½ teaspoon red pepper flakes, ¼ teaspoon salt, and pinch of black pepper until well combined.

4. Working with one meatball at a time, roll the meatball in the flour to lightly coat it, gently tapping off any excess. Transfer the flour-coated meatball to the egg mixture and coat on all sides so that there are no visible flour spots. Finally, generously coat the meatball in the bread-crumb mixture. Place on the prepared baking sheet. Repeat with the remaining meatballs. Spray the meatballs all over with cooking spray to help them crisp as they bake.

5. Bake for about 20 minutes, or until golden brown and crisp. Remove from the oven. Set a rack in the middle of the oven, then turn the oven to broil.

6. Scoop 1 teaspoon of marinara sauce on top of each meatball, then top the sauce with a mozzarella half. Return the meatballs to the oven and broil for 2 to 3 minutes, until the cheese is melty and bubbling brown in spots.

Toppings

½ cup (120 ml) thick marinara sauce, plus more for serving

10 mini mozzarella balls (ciliegine), sliced in half

Finely grated Parmesan, for garnishing

Chopped fresh basil, for garnishing

7. Garnish the meatballs with grated Parmesan and chopped basil and serve with more marinara sauce for dipping.

Note

The meatballs can be made 2 to 3 days in advance through step 5. Store in an airtight container in the refrigerator, then heat in the oven at 350°F (180°C; gas mark 4) for 10 minutes. Proceed with steps 6 and 7.

Holiday Bites

Make the holidays even more memorable with these savory and sweet festive bites that bring whimsical designs and seasonal flavors to your celebrations! From Love Bug Bites for Valentine's Day and Mummy Meatballs for Halloween to Candy Cane & Snowman Caprese Bites for Christmas and Midnight Kiss Cookie Bites for New Year's Eve, these brilliant bites are all so simple yet spectacular and sure to become tasty traditions you'll want to enjoy again and again.

Birthday Cake Cookie Bites with Party Hats

MAKES
60
BITES

These festive bites are a fun alternative to cake! Looking and tasting just like nostalgic birthday cake, the cookie bites are easily made with store-bought cake mix and lots of sprinkles. Pair them with these cute little party hats to make the celebration even sweeter.

Birthday Cake Cookie Bites

1 box (15.25 ounces, or 425 g) vanilla cake mix

½ cup (1 stick, or 115 g) unsalted butter, softened

2 large eggs

¾ cup (150 g) rainbow sprinkles, divided

1 container (12 ounces, or 340 g) whipped vanilla frosting

Party Hats

1 container (3 ounces, or 85 g) rainbow nonpareils

1 package (16 ounces, or 454 g) vanilla white candy coating

60 Original Bugles

1. **To make 60 birthday cake cookie bites:** In the bowl of a stand mixer fitted with the paddle attachment, beat the cake mix, softened butter, and eggs on low until well combined. (You can also beat by hand or use a hand mixer.) Fold in ½ cup (100 g) of the sprinkles. Cover the dough with plastic wrap and refrigerate for at least 1 hour.

2. Preheat the oven to 350°F (180°C; gas mark 4). Line two baking sheets with parchment paper (or bake in batches).

3. Roll the chilled dough into sixty 1 teaspoon–size balls, placing them about 1 inch (2.5 cm) apart on the prepared baking sheets. Bake for 8 minutes, or until they just start to crack on top. Let cool for a few minutes on the baking sheets, then transfer to a wire rack to cool completely. Spread the frosting on the cooled cookies and decorate with the remaining sprinkles.

4. **To make 60 party hats:** Line a baking sheet with parchment paper. Pour the nonpareils into a shallow bowl. Set both aside.

5. Melt the candy coating according to the package directions. Once melted, take one Bugle at a time, holding it by the pointy tip, and dip the bottom into the melted candy coating, then immediately dip into the nonpareils to create a ring around the wide end. Lay on the prepared baking sheet to dry, about 5 minutes. Repeat with the remaining Bugles.

6. Once the coating is set, hold the wide sprinkled end of each Bugle and dip only the pointy end into the melted candy coating, then immediately dip into the nonpareils. Set back on the parchment to dry while you finish the rest. Let set for at least 5 minutes.

Note

Frosted or unfrosted cookies can be made up to 3 days and party hats up to 5 days in advance. In separate airtight containers, store frosted cookies in the refrigerator and unfrosted cookies and party hats at room temperature.

Love Bug Bites

These cute bites are loveable and oh-so delicious! Easily created with red velvet cake mix and a variety of Valentine's sprinkles and candies, these love bugs are great for a Valentine's Day activity or party treat and will surely elicit lots of giggles and grins.

1 box (15.25 ounces, or 425 g) red velvet cake mix

¼ cup (60 g) vanilla frosting

28 Pocky Strawberry Cream Covered Biscuit Sticks

1 package (12 ounces, or 340 g) red candy coating melts

42 red jumbo heart-shaped sprinkles

84 pink jumbo heart-shaped sprinkles, divided

¼ cup (60 g) Valentine nonpareils

84 candy eyeballs

84 conversation hearts candies

1. Bake the cake mix according to the package directions for a 13 x 9-inch (33 x 23 cm) cake (using additional ingredients called for on the box, such as oil, water, and eggs). Let the cake cool completely.

2. In the bowl of a stand mixer fitted with the paddle attachment, crumble in the cooled cake along with the frosting. Beat on medium speed until the cake starts to come together. (You can also use a hand mixer.) Roll the mixture into 42 heaping 1 tablespoon-size balls and place on a parchment-lined baking sheet. Place the baking sheet in the refrigerator for at least 30 minutes.

3. Meanwhile, make the antennae by cutting the pink portion of each of the Pocky sticks into three 1-inch (2.5 cm) pieces.

4. In a shallow microwave-safe bowl, melt the candy coating according to the package directions. Dip one end of each pink stick piece barely into the melted candy coating and attach 48 each of the red and pink heart-shaped sprinkles until you have 84 antennae.

5. Line another baking sheet with parchment paper. Remove the cake balls from the refrigerator and coat them, one at a time, in the melted candy coating, using a fork to gently roll each cake ball in it. Try to keep some candy coating between the cake ball and the fork at all times to maintain a smooth coating and the round shape of the cake ball. Carefully lift out the cake bite and let the excess candy coating drip off before placing it on the prepared baking sheet.

6. Immediately sprinkle each coated cake bite with the nonpareils, then stick 2 antennae into the top. Press 2 candy eyeballs into the front and a pink heart-shaped sprinkle below the eyes for the nose. Stick 2 conversation hearts, pointy sides in, at the base of each love bug for the feet. (If the candy coating starts to harden before you have finished, use some of the reserved melted candy coating to attach the decorations to it.)

7. Allow the love bugs to set completely, then break off any excess candy coating that may have gathered around the bottom of the ball.

Note

These bites can be made in advance and stored in an airtight container for up to 3 days at room temperature or up to 1 week in the refrigerator.

King Cake Bites

This quick twist on a traditional king cake is perfect for celebrating Mardi Gras! All you need are canned cinnamon rolls and yellow, purple, and green sugars to bring these together for an easy and delicious Fat Tuesday treat. You could also switch up the colors of the sugars to make these tasty bites fit any occasion.

1 can (17.5 ounces, or 496 g) refrigerated jumbo cinnamon rolls with original icing (5 count; such as Pillsbury Grands!)

1 tablespoon yellow sparkling sugar

1 tablespoon purple sparkling sugar

1 tablespoon green sparkling sugar

1. Preheat the oven to 350°F (180°C; gas mark 4). Line a baking sheet with parchment paper.

2. Unroll each cinnamon roll into a long strip. Cut each strip lengthwise into 4 smaller strips, 4 to 5 inches (10 to 12.5 cm) long, so that you have 20 strips total.

3. Twist each strip of dough into a spiral, then shape into a small circle, pressing the ends together so that the bites hold their circular shape as they bake. Place on the prepared baking sheet a few inches (7.5 cm) apart.

4. Bake for 15 minutes, or until golden brown.

5. Heat the icing for about 10 seconds in the microwave, then drizzle over the top of the hot bites. Immediately sprinkle the icing with the yellow, purple, and green sugars, making sure each color covers a third of each bite.

Note

These bites can be made up to 2 days in advance. Cover with plastic wrap and store in an airtight container at room temperature.

Pot o' Gold Rainbow & Shamrock Pretzel Bites

MAKES
24
BITES

Everyone will be feelin' lucky to get to eat these festive treats! They're cute and crafty and sure to sweeten up any Saint Patrick's Day celebration. The sweet-and-salty flavors paired with the chewy-and-crunchy textures make them oh-so fun to enjoy.

Pot o' Gold Rainbow Pretzel Bites

12 waffle-shaped pretzels

12 ROLO candies, unwrapped

2 tablespoons gold confetti sprinkles

12 Airhead Xtremes Rainbow Berry Bites

Shamrock Pretzel Bites

36 mini pretzel twists

6 thin pretzel sticks, broken in half

12 ROLO candies, unwrapped

1 tablespoon green sparkling sugar

12 green Milk Chocolate M&M'S

1. Preheat the oven to 250°F (120°C; gas mark ½). Line two baking sheets with parchment paper (or bake in batches).

2. **To make 12 pot o' gold rainbow pretzel bites:** Place the waffle-shaped pretzels in a single layer on one of the prepared baking sheets, then place a ROLO on the center of each pretzel.

3. Bake for 2 to 3 minutes, until the ROLOs just begin to soften but not melt. Remove from the oven and immediately sprinkle the gold confetti sprinkles over the softened ROLOs. Lean a rainbow bite against the softened candy on each bite so that it sticks to it.

4. Let the pretzel bites set until the chocolate is firm again.

5. **To make 12 shamrock pretzel bites:** On the remaining prepared baking sheet, arrange 3 mini pretzel twists and a pretzel stick half in the shape of a shamrock to make 12 shamrock shapes. Place a ROLO on the center of each shamrock shape where the pretzels all meet.

6. Bake for 2 to 3 minutes, until the ROLOs just begin to soften but not melt. Remove from the oven and immediately sprinkle the green sparkling sugar over the softened ROLOs, then gently press a green M&M into the center of each ROLO so that it melts down slightly to connect all the pretzels.

7. Let the pretzel bites set until the chocolate is firm again and the shamrocks hold their shapes when lifted.

Note

These bites can be prepped up to 1 week in advance. Store in an airtight container at room temperature.

Bunny Cookie Bites

MAKES
24
BITES

Every-*bunny* is going to love these bites! These bunny faces and behinds are as adorable as can be and would make for such a fun kids' activity for Easter. They are easily created with vanilla wafer cookies, frosting, and as many festive embellishments as your little bunny hearts' desire.

Cookies

24 regular vanilla wafer cookies

24 mini vanilla wafer cookies

¼ cup (60 g) white frosting

¼ cup (60 g) strawberry frosting

Decorations

Hot pink sparkling sugar

Light pink sparkling sugar

6 regular marshmallows, for bunny ears

Mini heart-shaped sprinkles

Mini white sugar pearl sprinkles

Mini pink sugar pearl sprinkles

Jumbo heart-shaped sprinkles

12 mini marshmallows, for bunny tails

1. **To prep the cookies:** Spread the tops of all the regular and mini cookies with a little white or strawberry frosting.

2. **To decorate the bunny faces:** Place the hot pink and light pink sparkling sugars in separate small bowls. Use kitchen scissors to cut each regular marshmallow into quarters, then immediately press the sticky side of each piece into hot pink or light pink sugar.

3. Attach 2 sprinkled marshmallow pieces, sprinkled sides up, on top of 12 regular frosted cookies for the ears. Place 2 mini heart-shaped sprinkles for the eyes and a white or pink pearl sprinkle for the nose.

4. **To decorate the bunny butts:** Decorate the 24 frosted mini cookies with mini and jumbo heart-shaped sprinkles and white and pink pearl sprinkles to look like bunny paws.

5. Attach 2 bunny paws at the bottom of the remaining 12 regular frosted cookies. Press a mini marshmallow into the center of each of the regular cookies for the bunny tails.

Note

These bites can be prepped a few hours in advance. Cover loosely with plastic wrap and store at room temperature. They should also be enjoyed within a few hours of decorating or the cookies will get soft.

Muffins with Mom,
Mini Muffins Many Ways

These mini muffins are a sweet way to celebrate Mother's Day and tell Mom you'd be *muffin* without her! They will make not only Mom but everyone else happy with their fun and flexible mix-ins. Quick and easy to prepare, they bake into soft, tasty breakfast treats.

Mini Muffins

Nonstick cooking spray, for greasing

1 cup (125 g) all-purpose flour

½ cup (100 g) granulated sugar

1 teaspoon baking powder

1 egg, lightly beaten

½ cup (120 ml) milk

1 teaspoon vanilla extract

2 tablespoons unsalted butter, melted

Mix-In Options

Chopped raspberries

Chopped strawberries

Small or chopped blueberries

Chopped bananas

Chopped nuts

Rainbow sprinkles

Mini chocolate chips

1. Preheat the oven to 350°F (180°C; gas mark 4). Spray a 24-cup mini muffin pan with cooking spray.

2. In a large bowl, whisk together the flour, sugar, and baking powder until well combined. Make a space in the center of the flour mixture and add the egg, milk, and vanilla. Whisk until just combined, then gently whisk in the melted butter until the batter is well combined.

3. Scoop the batter evenly among the prepared muffin cups, filling each one halfway full.

4. Place about 1 teaspoon of a mix-in on top of the batter in each muffin cup, combining some, if you desire, like the bananas and nuts. Use a chopstick or toothpick to stir the mix-ins into the muffin batter.

5. Bake for 15 to 18 minutes, until the muffins have risen and a toothpick inserted into the centers comes out clean. Let cool in the pan for 10 minutes before transferring to a wire rack to cool completely.

Note

These bites can be made up to 3 days in advance. Store the cooled muffins in an airtight container in the refrigerator. They can be enjoyed cold or at room temperature, or microwave for 15 seconds.

Donuts with Dad,
Maple Bacon Donut Bites

These bites are a decadent and delicious way to tell Dad you *donut* know what you'd do without him on Father's Day—and every day! And what more could a dad wish for than waking up on his special day to warm, flaky donuts and donut holes with a maple glaze and loads of crispy bacon.

Maple Bacon Glaze

5 slices maple–black pepper bacon

1 cup (125 g) powdered sugar

3 tablespoons maple syrup

1 tablespoon milk

Donuts

Canola oil, for deep-frying

1 can (6 ounces, or 170 g) refrigerated regular-size flaky layer biscuits (5 count)

1. **To make the maple bacon glaze:** Cook the bacon according to the package directions or until crisp, then transfer to a paper towel–lined plate to drain. Let cool completely before crumbling it into small pieces.

2. In a small bowl, whisk together the powdered sugar, maple syrup, and milk until smooth and of drizzling consistency.

3. **To make the donuts:** Pour the oil into a large, deep pan to a depth of at least 2 inches (5 cm) and heat over medium heat for about 5 minutes, or until the oil temperature reaches 350°F (180°C). Line a baking sheet with foil, then set a wire baking rack on the baking sheet.

4. While the oil heats, peel each biscuit in half crosswise. Lay each biscuit half on a cutting board and, using a 1-inch (2.5 cm) round biscuit or cookie cutter, cut the center out of each biscuit. You will get 2 donuts and 2 donut holes from each biscuit.

5. Cooking in batches, drop the dough rings and holes into the hot oil, watching carefully and turning when golden, 1 to 2 minutes per side. Once the donuts are golden on both sides, transfer to the prepared rack.

6. Dip the top of each donut and donut hole into the maple glaze and let any excess drip back into the bowl. Place the glazed donuts back onto the rack, glazed sides up, and sprinkle generously with the bacon pieces.

Note

These bites can be made up to 2 days in advance, but they are best enjoyed the same day, either warm or at room temperature. Cover loosely with plastic wrap and store at room temperature.

Patriotic Pie Bites

There's nothing more American than pie, right?! Whether you love apple, blueberry, or cherry pie, these star-spangled sweeties will satisfy all the pie cravings at your party. They're a cute and clever way to serve dessert at any patriotic celebration.

Patriotic Pie Bites

Nonstick cooking spray, for greasing

1 box (14.1 ounces, or 399 g) refrigerated piecrusts (2 piecrusts), thawed

Flour, for dusting

½ cup (130 g) prepared blueberry pie filling

¾ cup (195 g) prepared cherry pie filling

¾ cup (195 g) prepared apple pie filling (if the apple pieces are large, chop up the filling)

Whipped cream, for topping (optional)

Supplies

1-inch (2.5 cm) star-shaped cookie cutter

1. Preheat the oven to 375°F (190°C; gas mark 5). Spray a 24-cup mini muffin pan with cooking spray.

2. Unfold one thawed piecrust at a time on a lightly floured surface. With a 2½-inch (6 cm) round biscuit or cookie cutter, cut 24 rounds from the piecrusts. Using the cookie cutter, cut 6 mini star shapes from the extra dough for garnishing the blueberry pies.

3. Press a round of piecrust into the bottom and up the sides of each prepared muffin cup. Lay the prepared muffin pan horizontally in front of you and fill the crusts to look like an American flag as follows: top row, 3 blueberry and 3 cherry; second row, 3 blueberry and 3 apple; third row, all cherry; and bottom row, all apple.

4. Top each blueberry pie with a mini star-shaped piece of dough.

5. Bake for 25 to 30 minutes, until the filling begins to bubble and set in the center and the crusts turn golden brown around the edges.

6. Allow to cool for 10 minutes or so before removing from the pan and recreating the flag shape on a platter.

7. Top the apple pie bites with a dollop of whipped cream (if using).

Note

These bites can be made in advance and stored in an airtight container for up to 2 days at room temperature or up to 4 days in the refrigerator.

Jack-o'-Lantern Mac 'n' Cheese Bites

MAKES
12
BITES

Now this is how you have fun with your food on Halloween! Spookily cute and oh-so scrumptious, these cheesy bites make for a savory start to what is sure to be a very sweet night.

1 cup (112 g) elbow macaroni

2 tablespoons unsalted butter

2 tablespoons all-purpose flour

½ teaspoon kosher salt

¾ cup (180 ml) milk

2 cups (230 g) shredded Cheddar, divided

Nonstick cooking spray, for greasing

1 large egg, beaten

12 pepperoni slices

12 small broccoli florets, steamed

Note

These bites can be made up to 3 days in advance. Store in an airtight container in the refrigerator, then reheat in the oven at 300°F (150°C; gas mark 2) until heated through or in the microwave for about 30 seconds each.

1. Cook the macaroni according to the package directions. Drain.

2. In a medium pot, melt the butter over medium heat. Whisk in the flour and salt until the mixture is thick and starts to turn light brown. Slowly pour in the milk and continue to whisk until bubbling and thick, about 3 minutes. Add 1½ cups (170 g) of the shredded cheese and stir until melted. Remove the pan from the heat and stir in the cooked macaroni until well combined. Set aside to cool for 15 minutes.

3. Preheat the oven to 375°F (190°C; gas mark 5). Spray a 12-cup muffin pan with nonstick cooking spray.

4. Stir the beaten egg into the cooled macaroni and cheese until well incorporated, then divide the macaroni and cheese evenly among the prepared muffin cups, filling each cup about one-third full. Top each bite with some of the remaining shredded cheese, covering each one completely.

5. Bake for 15 minutes, or until the cheese melts and the edges of each bite start to crisp. Let the bites cool in the pan for 10 minutes before transferring to a platter. If necessary, run a knife around the edge of each bite to easily release them from the pan.

6. Using a sharp knife, cut the pepperoni slices into various shapes for the jack-o'-lantern faces. Decorate the top of each bite with the pepperoni shapes. Stick a steamed broccoli floret into the top of each bite for the stem.

7. Serve immediately, or keep warm in a 200°F (95°C; gas mark ¼) oven until ready to serve.

(See photograph on pages 70–71)

Mummy Meatballs

It's a wrap! You won't need to do much more when entertaining for Halloween if you serve these adorably creepy meatballs.

24 fresh uncooked Italian-style meatballs (2 tablespoon–size) or 1 pound (454 g) seasoned ground meatball mixture

48 large fettuccine noodles

2 cups (480 ml) marinara sauce

2 tablespoons whole-milk ricotta

3 large pitted black olives, cut into 48 tiny circles, for the pupils

1. Preheat the oven to 375°F (190°C; gas mark 5). If using meatball mixture, form it into twenty-four 2 tablespoon–size meatballs.

2. Cook the fettuccine noodles to al dente according to the package directions, then drain. Let cool a bit before handling in the next step.

3. Wrap 2 cooked fettuccine noodles around each meatball, tucking the pasta ends into each other to secure them around the meatballs. Pour the marinara sauce into the bottom of an 8-inch (20 cm) baking dish, then arrange the meatballs on top of the marinara sauce.

4. Bake for 15 minutes, or until the meatballs are cooked through and the pasta starts to slightly crisp all over.

5. When the meatballs come out of the oven, place the ricotta in a resealable plastic bag and make a small snip off one of the corners. Squeeze 2 dollops of ricotta onto the top of each meatball, then place a black olive circle on the center of each dollop of ricotta for the mummy eyes.

6. Serve immediately, or keep warm in a 200°F (95°C; gas mark ¼) oven until ready to serve.

Notes

- These bites can be prepped a day in advance through step 3 to the point of baking. Store in the baking dish, covered with the lid or plastic wrap, in the refrigerator, then proceed with steps 4 through 6.

- To make an olive spider, slice a whole pitted black olive in half lengthwise. Place one-half on a platter for the body of the spider, then thinly slice the other half crosswise into 6 or 8 slices, depending on the size of the olive, for the spider's legs. Place 3 or 4 legs on each side of the spider's body.

(See photograph on pages 70–71)

Monster Cookie Balls

These mischievous little monsters are no-bake and so fun to make! Perfect for a Halloween party when you want to serve something that's sweet but a little healthier, these bites are loaded with all the yumminess of a good monster cookie—peanut butter, oats, honey, and chocolate.

1 cup (256 g) crunchy peanut butter

½ cup (120 ml) honey

1 teaspoon vanilla extract

2½ cups (215 g) quick oats

½ cup (90 g) mini chocolate chips

½ cup (80 g) orange and brown Milk Chocolate M&M'S Minis

½ cup (75 g) monster-colored Halloween sprinkles (orange, black, purple, and green mix)

90 candy eyeballs

1. Line a baking sheet with parchment paper.

2. In a large bowl, stir together the peanut butter, honey, and vanilla until well combined.

3. Stir in the oats until well combined.

4. Add the mini chocolate chips, M&M'S Minis, and sprinkles. Stir to combine well.

5. Using clean hands, roll the mixture into 1 tablespoon–size smooth balls and place on the prepared baking sheet.

6. Press 3 candy eyeballs into the top and/or sides of each bite.

7. Place the bites in the refrigerator for at least 30 minutes before serving.

Note

These bites can be made up to 1 week in advance. Store in an airtight container in the refrigerator.

Pumpkin Pie Bites

Once you make these no-bake bites, you may never make a traditional pumpkin pie again! Perfect for serving during any fall festivities, these bites will have everyone raving over how cute they are and how they taste just like, well, pumpkin pie.

1 package (8 ounces, or 227 g) cream cheese, softened

¾ cup (95 g) powdered sugar

¼ cup (55 g) canned 100% pure pumpkin

1 teaspoon pumpkin pie spice

1 teaspoon vanilla extract

2½ cups (300 g) fine graham cracker crumbs, divided

20 semisweet chocolate chips

20 white chocolate chips

1. In the bowl of a stand mixer fitted with the paddle attachment, beat the cream cheese and powdered sugar on medium until well combined and smooth. (You can also use a hand mixer.) Add the pumpkin, pumpkin pie spice, and vanilla and beat on medium until well incorporated.

2. Stir in 2 cups (240 g) of the graham cracker crumbs, then cover with plastic wrap and refrigerate the mixture for at least 1 hour.

3. Place the remaining ½ cup (60 g) graham cracker crumbs in a shallow bowl. Scoop half of the chilled mixture into twenty 1 tablespoon–size balls for pumpkin shapes, then roll each ball in the graham cracker crumbs to coat.

4. Use a toothpick to make lines around the balls so that they look like little pumpkins, then press a semisweet chocolate chip into the top of each one for the stem.

5. Shape the remaining mixture into twenty 1 tablespoon–size wedges that look like pie slices, then roll each wedge in the remaining graham cracker crumbs to coat.

6. Top each pie-slice bite with a white chocolate chip for the whipped cream.

7. Return the bites to the refrigerator for at least 30 minutes, or until ready to serve.

Note

These bites can be made up to 2 weeks in advance. Store in an airtight container in the refrigerator, then enjoy cold.

Thanksgiving Cracker Bites

Everyone is sure to gobble up this adorable cast of Thanksgiving bites! With turkeys, pumpkins, and cornucopias—oh my!—they're a fun preshow for the big event.

Cheese Spread

8 ounces (227 g) cream cheese, softened

1 cup (115 g) shredded sharp white Cheddar

¼ cup (30 g) crushed pecans

¼ cup (55 g) real bacon bits

¼ cup (15 g) chopped green onion

½ teaspoon kosher salt

36 round crackers

Cornucopias

12 Original Bugles

12 whole pecans, coarsely chopped

12 thinly sliced almonds, coarsely chopped

12 dried cranberries, coarsely chopped

12 dried apricots, coarsely chopped

1 tablespoon chopped fresh rosemary

Pumpkins

¼ cup (30 g) finely shredded orange Cheddar (1 teaspoon per cracker)

3 sprigs fresh rosemary, separated into 12 mini sprigs

Turkeys

36 whole pecans

48 thinly sliced almonds

24 dried cranberries

3 dried apricots, quartered

1. **To make the cheese spread:** In a large bowl, stir together the cream cheese, shredded white Cheddar, crushed pecans, bacon bits, green onion, and salt until well combined. Use immediately, or cover loosely with plastic wrap and refrigerate until ready to assemble the cracker bites.

2. Place the crackers in a single layer on a platter or work surface. Spread a thick layer of the cheese spread onto each cracker.

3. **To assemble the cornucopias:** Stick a Bugle into the cheese spread on the center of the top edge of 12 crackers with the pointed tip sticking up and toward you. Press some chopped pecans, almonds, dried cranberries, and dried apricots into the cheese spread around and in front of the wide end of the Bugle. Garnish with the rosemary.

4. **To assemble the pumpkins:** Press about 1 teaspoon of shredded orange Cheddar into the cheese spread on 12 crackers. Place a mini sprig of rosemary on the top center of each cracker for the stem.

5. **To assemble the turkeys:** For the turkey feathers, stand up and press 3 whole pecans into the cheese spread along the top edge of each of the remaining 12 crackers, then stand up and press 4 sliced almonds in front of the pecans. Place 2 dried cranberries for the eyes and a dried apricot quarter, pointed side down, for the snood.

Note

These bites can be assembled up to 3 hours in advance. Cover loosely with plastic wrap and store in the refrigerator.

Candy Cane & Snowman Caprese Bites

It doesn't get any cuter than these caprese bites! Deliciously festive, the snowmen are more traditional in flavor, while the candy canes are also shrimp cocktail. When you put these out on the holiday table, everyone will ooh and aah over them and think they're almost too adorable to eat . . . almost.

Candy Cane Caprese Bites

2 tablespoons olive oil

1 clove garlic, minced

1 tablespoon dried Italian seasoning

24 cooked cocktail shrimp, tails removed

24 mini mozzarella balls (ciliegine)

24 cherry tomatoes, cut in half crosswise

24 small leaves fresh basil

Snowman Caprese Bites

52 mini mozzarella balls (ciliegine), divided

6 petite baby carrots

6 large pitted whole black olives

12 cherry tomatoes, cut in half crosswise

24 small leaves fresh basil

For Serving

Cocktail sauce

Pesto

Festive crackers or toasted baguette slices (optional)

Supplies

48 decorative food picks

1. **To make the candy cane caprese bites:** In a small bowl, whisk together the olive oil, garlic, and Italian seasoning. Brush the olive oil mixture all over the shrimp.

2. Cut the rounded ends off each mozzarella ball, then slice the remaining cheese in half crosswise.

3. **To assemble:** On a food pick, place a mini mozzarella half, a cherry tomato half, another mini mozzarella half, another cherry tomato half, and a basil leaf, leaving enough room to stick a shrimp on top for the candy-cane look. Attach only the bottom portion of the shrimp to the food pick so that the curved portion is sticking up. Repeat with the remaining ingredients.

4. **To make the snowman caprese bites:** Cut 4 mini mozzarella balls each into 6 smaller pieces for the hat tops.

5. Cut each carrot into 4 smaller pieces with a pointy end for noses.

6. Slice the black olives into 96 tiny circles for the eyes and buttons.

7. **To assemble:** On a food pick, place a tiny piece of mozzarella, a cherry tomato half (sliced side down), a mozzarella ball, a basil leaf, and another mozzarella ball. Repeat with the remaining ingredients.

8. Lay a snowman down and use a toothpick to make tiny holes for the eyes, nose, and buttons. Press olive pieces into the holes for the eyes and buttons and press a pointed carrot piece into the hole for the nose. Repeat with the remaining ingredients.

9. Serve the candy canes with cocktail sauce and the snowmen with pesto for dipping, along with crackers or baguette slices (if using).

Note

These bites can be assembled a day in advance. Store in an airtight container in the refrigerator.

Santa Hat & Rudolph Pancake Bites

You're sure to see lots of smiles on Christmas morning when you serve these jolly and joyful pancake bites made to look like Santa hats and Rudolph! Let the kids help turn classic pancake batter and decorations into these cute creations.

Pancake Batter

½ cup (1 stick, or 115 g) unsalted butter, melted and slightly cooled

¼ cup (60 ml) maple syrup

1 cup (240 ml) milk

2 large eggs

1 teaspoon vanilla extract

1 cup (130 g) all-purpose flour

1 teaspoon baking soda

Santa Hat Pancake Bites

4 large bananas

30 large, pointed strawberries

Nonstick cooking spray, for greasing

30 mini marshmallows

Rudolph Pancake Bites

Nonstick cooking spray, for greasing

1½ cups (340 g) peanut butter

8 slices bacon, cooked to medium crisp

24 raspberries

For Serving

Powdered sugar

Maple syrup

Supplies

30 decorative food picks

1. **To make the pancake batter:** Add the melted butter to a large bowl, then whisk in the maple syrup followed by the milk, eggs, and vanilla. Stir in the flour and baking soda until well combined. Evenly divide the batter between two bowls.

2. **To make 30 Santa hat pancake bites:** Slice the bananas into sixty ¼-inch-thick (6 mm) slices. Slice the stem off each strawberry, then cut a ¼-inch-thick (6 mm) slice from the top of each strawberry and reserve them, leaving the pointed portion.

3. Lightly grease a large skillet with nonstick cooking spray and heat over medium heat. Once the skillet is hot, dip each banana slice into the batter in one of the bowls and let the excess drip off. Add the pancake batter–covered bananas to the skillet, in batches, and cook until you see bubbles start to form on the edges, about 1 minute. Flip and cook on the other side for 1 minute, or until light brown on both sides and completely cooked around the edges.

4. **To assemble:** On a work surface, stack a pancake, then a reserved slice of strawberry, another pancake, and a pointed strawberry. Top with a mini marshmallow, then secure with a food pick.

5. **To make 24 Rudolph pancake bites:** Lightly grease the same skillet with nonstick cooking spray and heat over medium heat. Once the skillet is hot, pour enough batter from the other bowl into the pan to make an 8-inch (20 cm) round pancake. Let cook until bubbles start to form on top, about 45 seconds. Flip and cook on the other side for 30 to 45 seconds, until golden brown on both sides. You want to make sure the pancake is not too crisp and easy to fold. Repeat with the remaining batter to make 4 large pancakes total.

6. **To assemble:** Spread a thin layer of peanut butter onto one side of each pancake, then roll up the pancakes. Using a sharp knife, cut the ends off the pancake rolls, then slice each roll into 6 equal-size pieces, about 1 inch (2.5 cm) thick, for 24 rolls total. Insert the tip of the knife into the top of each roll in two places, about ¼ inch (6 mm) deep, to hold the bacon antlers.

7. Cut each slice of bacon in half lengthwise, then cut each half into 3 equal-size strips crosswise so that you have 48 smaller strips. Push a strip of bacon into each slit in the top of each roll-up. Carefully push a raspberry into the center of each roll-up for the red nose.

8. Serve the Santa hats and Rudolphs immediately, or cover loosely with plastic wrap and refrigerate until ready to serve. Dust with powdered sugar and serve with maple syrup for dipping. They can be enjoyed warm, at room temperature, or cold.

Bow-Tie Antipasto Bites

MAKES **40** BITES

These charming bites are dressed to impress! A bow tie, even in pasta form, is quite elegant and, when topping olives, salami, and cheese, quite delicious. Not only for New Year's Eve, these bites are a fabulous addition to any special occasion.

Bow-Tie Antipasto Bites

40 pieces bow-tie pasta

1 tablespoon olive oil

½ teaspoon garlic salt

1 teaspoon dried Italian seasoning

1 block (7 ounces, or 198 g) aged white Cheddar (about a 3½-inch, or 9-cm, square)

20 large pimiento-stuffed green olives

20 large pitted whole black olives

40 peppered salami slices

Supplies

40 decorative food picks

1. Cook the pasta to al dente according to the package directions. Drain and let dry, then toss with the olive oil, garlic salt, and Italian seasoning.

2. Slice the cheese into forty ¾-inch (2 cm) blocks that are ½ inch (1 cm) thick.

3. To assemble, on a food pick, place a piece of bow-tie pasta, an olive—either green or black—a folded slice of salami, and a block of cheese. Repeat with the remaining ingredients.

Note

These bites can be assembled up to 2 days in advance. Store in an airtight container in the refrigerator.

Midnight Kiss Cookie Bites

MAKES
24
BITES

Ring in the New Year with these dazzling bites! Why not get your kiss when the clock strikes midnight with one of these decadent cookies. The dark chocolate makes them irresistibly rich and the gold and silver sprinkles make them party perfect.

½ cup (1 stick, or 115 g) unsalted butter, softened

¾ cup (150 g) granulated sugar

1 large egg

1 teaspoon vanilla extract

1 cup (125 g) all-purpose flour

⅓ cup (30 g) dark cocoa powder

½ teaspoon kosher salt

¼ cup (60 g) gold sparkling sugar

¼ cup (60 g) silver sparkling sugar

¼ cup (60 g) clear sparkling sugar

24 Hershey's Kisses Special Dark Mildly Sweet Chocolate Candies

1. In the bowl of a stand mixer fitted with the paddle attachment, beat the butter and sugar on medium until well combined. (You can also beat by hand or use a hand mixer.) Add the egg and vanilla and beat on medium until well incorporated.

2. In a small bowl, whisk together the flour, cocoa powder, and salt until well combined.

3. Add the flour mixture to the butter mixture and beat on low until well combined and it comes together as a dough. Roll into a ball, wrap with plastic wrap, and place in the refrigerator for 1 hour, or until firm enough to handle.

4. Place the sparkling sugars in three separate shallow bowls or combine them in one bowl if you prefer.

5. Preheat the oven to 350°F (180°C; gas mark 4). Line two baking sheets with parchment paper (or bake in batches).

6. Shape the dough into twenty-four 1 tablespoon–size balls. Place the sparkling sugars in separate bowls and roll 8 balls in the gold sugar, 8 balls in the silver sugar, and 8 balls in the clear sugar. (You can also combine the sugars for rolling, if desired.) Place the sugar-coated balls of dough a few inches (7.5 cm) apart on the prepared baking sheets.

7. Bake for 10 minutes, or until set and just starting to crack on top. Meanwhile, remove the wrappers from the chocolate Kisses.

8. Once the cookies are baked, let them cool for just a minute, then quickly press a chocolate Kiss into the center of each cookie. Let cool completely on the baking sheets or a wire rack before serving.

Note

These bites can be made up to 5 days in advance. Store in an airtight container at room temperature.

Breakfast Bites

These brilliant bites are creative takes on breakfast classics that are perfect to grab and go on a busy weekday or enjoy during a leisurely brunch with family and friends! They are guaranteed to make anyone rise and shine with a smile to last all day. Whether you wake up craving something savory, such as Breakfast Burrito Roll-Up Bites, or something sweet, such as Blueberry Streusel Muffin-Top Bites, you're sure to love them. So, pour some coffee or juice and enjoy the best start to your day with these quick and delicious bites.

Pancake Taco Bites

Pancake party! These bites are a fun, handheld way to serve pancakes. A breakfast great is made even more enjoyable when filled with all the yummy toppings your heart could desire. This is a tasty, customizable treat that everyone will be thrilled to wake up to.

Pancakes

¼ cup (½ stick, or 55 g) unsalted butter, melted and slightly cooled

2 tablespoons maple syrup, plus more for serving

½ cup (120 ml) milk

1 large egg

½ teaspoon vanilla extract

½ cup (65 g) all-purpose flour

½ teaspoon baking soda

Nonstick cooking spray, for greasing

Filling Options

Chocolate hazelnut spread

Peanut butter

Jelly

Yogurt

Whipped cream

Chopped strawberries

Chopped bananas

Chopped raspberries

Chopped blueberries

Mini marshmallows

Mini chocolate chips

Chopped nuts

Slivered almonds

Granola

Sprinkles

1. **To make the pancakes:** Add the melted butter to a large bowl, then whisk in the maple syrup followed by the milk, egg, and vanilla. Stir in the flour and baking soda until well combined.

2. Lightly grease a large skillet or griddle with nonstick cooking spray and heat over medium heat. Cooking in batches, scoop 1 tablespoon–size portions of batter onto the skillet and spread into a 2½-inch (6 cm) circle. Let cook until you see bubbles start to form on top, about 45 seconds. Flip and cook on the other side for 30 to 45 seconds, until golden brown on both sides. You want to make sure the pancakes are not too crisp and easy to fold.

3. **To assemble:** Spread one side of a pancake with a thin layer of chocolate hazelnut spread, peanut butter, jelly, yogurt, and/or whipped cream. Fill with chopped fruit, if desired, then sprinkle with marshmallows, chocolate chips, nuts, granola, and/or sprinkles.

4. Serve with maple syrup for dipping.

Note

The pancakes can be made up to 2 days in advance. Store in an airtight bag in the refrigerator, then let them come to room temperature before filling and folding into a taco. Once filled, they should be enjoyed immediately.

Eggs Benedict Bites

These charming little Bennies are sure to be the stars of your brunch spread! They look like they're straight out of the kitchen of a chic brunch spot but can easily be made and enjoyed in the comfort of your own home. This is a Sunday brunch standard to truly enjoy one bite at a time.

Eggs Benedict

Nonstick cooking spray, for greasing

24 large eggs, yolks separated (reserve the egg whites for another use)

6 English muffins, halved

1 tablespoon canola oil

6 slices Canadian bacon

Hollandaise Butter

2 egg yolks

1 tablespoon fresh lemon juice, plus more to taste

6 tablespoons unsalted butter, softened, divided

Kosher salt, to taste

Garnishes

Flaky sea salt

Ground black pepper

Paprika

2 tablespoons finely chopped green onion

Note

The hollandaise butter can be made up to 2 days in advance. Store in an airtight container in the refrigerator, then let soften before using.

1. **To make the eggs Benedict:** Preheat the oven to 350°F (180°C; gas mark 4). Spray a 24-cup mini muffin pan with nonstick cooking spray.

2. Place an egg yolk in each prepared muffin cup and bake for 5 to 7 minutes, until the white rims around the yolks are set but the yolks are still runny. Let set in the pan for at least 5 minutes or until ready to assemble the bites. Run a spatula around the edges of the eggs and carefully remove from the pan. Increase the oven temperature to 400°F (200°C; gas mark 6).

3. Slightly flatten each English muffin half with a rolling pin or your hands to at least 4 inches (10 cm) wide. Use a 1½- to 2-inch (4 to 5 cm) round biscuit or cookie cutter to cut 2 circles out of each English muffin half. Place the rounds in a single layer on a baking sheet and toast in the oven for 8 to 10 minutes, until golden brown.

4. Meanwhile, in a large skillet, heat the oil over medium heat. Add the Canadian bacon slices and cook for 2 minutes, then turn and cook for 1 to 2 minutes longer, until lightly browned. Transfer to a paper towel–lined plate to drain, then cut each slice into quarters.

5. **To make the hollandaise butter:** In a large bowl, whisk together the 2 egg yolks and lemon juice until well combined. Melt 2 tablespoons of the butter in the microwave and immediately pour into the egg yolk mixture, whisking continuously until well combined. Whisk in the remaining 4 tablespoons butter (softened, not melted) until smooth and of spreading consistency. Season with kosher salt.

6. **To assemble:** Spread some of the hollandaise butter onto each muffin round, letting it drip over the sides slightly. Add a quarter of Canadian bacon and top with a cooked egg yolk. Sprinkle the bites with sea salt, pepper, and paprika and finish with some chopped green onion.

7. Serve immediately, or keep warm in a 200°F (95°C; gas mark ¼) oven until ready to serve and garnish the bites right before serving.

Cinnamon Sugar Cruffin Bites

Croissant meets muffin in these bites that combine the best of breakfast pastries! With layers of cinnamon sugar, this incredible pastry combo will make you think you're still dreaming.

Nonstick cooking spray, for greasing

½ cup (100 g) granulated sugar

2 tablespoons ground cinnamon

Flour, for dusting (optional)

2 cans (8 ounces, or 225 g, each) refrigerated crescent rolls (8 count each)

½ cup (1 stick, or 115 g) unsalted butter, softened

1. Preheat the oven to 350°F (180°C; gas mark 4). Spray a 24-cup mini muffin pan with nonstick cooking spray.

2. In a small bowl, whisk together the sugar and cinnamon. Reserve 2 tablespoons for tossing the cruffins in after they bake.

3. On a lightly floured or parchment-lined work surface, roll out each crescent dough sheet so that the perforated lines blend together and it measures about 15 x 8 inches (38 x 20 cm). Spread half of the softened butter onto each sheet of crescent dough. Sprinkle each sheet evenly with the cinnamon-sugar mixture.

4. Starting with a long end of one of the dough sheets, tightly roll up the dough into a log. Repeat with the second sheet of dough. Cut each log into three 5-inch (12.5 cm) sections so that you have 6 smaller logs total. Cut each of these logs in half lengthwise, then turn each half so that the layers are facedown on the work surface. Cut each section in half lengthwise again for 24 pieces total.

5. Stretch and wrap each piece around your index finger with the layered sides facing out to form the shape of a muffin. Place each cruffin in a prepared muffin cup.

6. Bake for 18 to 20 minutes, until golden brown on top, rotating the pan halfway through the baking time. Let set in the pan for 5 minutes. Add the reserved cinnamon-sugar mixture to a resealable plastic bag. Transfer the baked cruffins to the bag, seal, and shake to coat in the cinnamon sugar.

Note

These bites can be made up to 3 days in advance. Store in an airtight container at room temperature, then enjoy at room temperature or reheat in the oven at 350°F (180°C; gas mark 4) for about 5 minutes, or until crisp and warmed through.

Breakfast Burrito Roll-Up Bites

Roll out of bed to the most scrumptious and satisfying breakfast roll-ups! Filled with egg, bacon, avocado, cheese, and more, they're the best way to start the day.

Soft Scrambled Eggs

6 large eggs

½ teaspoon kosher salt

¼ cup (60 ml) milk

1 tablespoon unsalted butter

Burrito Roll-Ups

4 burrito-size flour tortillas (10 inches, or 25 cm)

1 large or 2 small avocados, mashed (1⅓ cups, or 290 g, mashed avocado)

1 cup (115 g) shredded Monterey Jack and Cheddar blend

12 slices cooked bacon, crumbled (¾ cup, or 165 g, total)

1 cup (240 g) pico de gallo

1 cup (130 g) refrigerated or frozen hash browns, cooked according to the package directions

4 tablespoons unsalted butter, divided

Salsa, for serving

Hot sauce, for serving

1. **To make the soft scrambled eggs:** In a large bowl, whisk the eggs with the salt and milk until pale yellow in color and no visible egg whites remain.

2. In a large skillet, melt the 1 tablespoon butter over medium-low heat. When the butter is barely bubbling, add the eggs and cook, gently folding and pushing them around with a spatula, until the eggs form soft curds and are just set. Remove from the heat.

3. **To make the burrito roll-ups:** Making one burrito at a time, microwave a tortilla for about 10 seconds. Spread with a quarter of the mashed avocado, then layer with a quarter each of the soft scrambled eggs, shredded cheese, crumbled bacon, pico de gallo, and cooked hash browns. Tightly roll the tortilla from one end to the other like a jelly roll.

4. In a large skillet, melt 1 tablespoon of the butter over medium heat. Add the rolled-up burrito to the skillet, seam side down, and sear on each side for about 2 minutes. Keep warm in a 200°F (95°C; gas mark ¼) oven while you repeat the filling, rolling, and searing for the remaining 3 burritos.

5. When ready to serve, cut off the ends of each burrito roll-up and then slice into 1-inch-thick (2.5 cm) rounds.

6. Serve immediately with salsa and hot sauce, or lay the burrito bites in a single layer on a parchment-lined baking sheet and keep warm in a 200°F (95°C; gas mark ¼) oven until ready to serve.

Note

These bites can be made up to 3 days in advance. Store in an airtight container in the refrigerator, then reheat in the microwave for 15 seconds each.

Dutch Baby Bites

MAKES **24** BITES

Oh, baby! Skip the skillet and use a mini muffin pan to make these fluffy, custardy pancakes. Topped with fresh berries and powdered sugar and served with maple syrup on the side for drizzling, they're sure to get mouths watering when you make them for breakfast or brunch.

Dutch Baby Bites

½ cup (65 g) all-purpose flour

½ cup (120 ml) whole milk

2 large eggs

2 tablespoons granulated sugar

½ teaspoon vanilla extract

¼ teaspoon kosher salt

¼ cup (½ stick, or 55 g) unsalted butter, melted

For Serving

Blueberries

Raspberries

Powdered sugar

Maple syrup

1. Preheat the oven to 400°F (200°C; gas mark 6) and place a 24-cup mini muffin pan on the middle rack of the oven to warm.

2. In a blender or food processor, blend the flour, milk, eggs, granulated sugar, vanilla, and salt into a smooth liquid, about 1 minute. Let the batter set for 10 minutes.

3. Carefully remove the muffin pan from the oven and set it on a rimmed baking sheet. Evenly divide the melted butter among the muffin cups. Scoop 1 tablespoon of batter into each muffin cup, filling it about halfway. The butter will settle around the batter.

4. Bake for 12 to 15 minutes, until puffed and golden brown on top. Let cool in the pan for a few minutes before removing.

5. Serve with berries and powdered sugar for topping and maple syrup for dipping.

Note

The batter can be made up to 12 hours in advance. Store in an airtight container in the refrigerator, then stir well before using.

Strawberry Toaster Pastry Bites

These are the cutest little bites you will ever see and eat! They are such a fun treat to serve for breakfast at a sleepover or birthday party. Kids—and kids at heart—will go wild over how fun and yummy these are.

Toaster Pastries

Flour, for dusting

1 refrigerated piecrust (9 inches, or 23 cm), at room temperature

1 tablespoon strawberry jam

2 tablespoons unsalted butter, melted, for brushing

Icing

½ cup (65 g) powdered sugar

1 tablespoon milk

2 tablespoons rainbow nonpareils, for garnishing

1. **To make the toaster pastries:** Preheat the oven to 400°F (200°C; gas mark 6). Line a baking sheet with parchment paper.

2. On a lightly floured cutting board, using a rolling pin, roll out the piecrust to a 9 x 8-inch (23 x 20 cm) rectangle. Fold the 9-inch (23 cm) side over to the other side so that it is layered.

3. Use a kitchen-use-only ruler to cut 1-inch-wide (2.5 cm) lines down the 8-inch (20 cm) length of the crust, then measure and cut 1½-inch-wide (4 cm) lines across the crust to create double stacks of twenty-four 1 x 1½-inch (2.5 x 4 cm) rectangles.

4. Working with each pair of crusts, open them up and scoop about ⅛ teaspoon of strawberry jam onto the center of one of the rectangles. Evenly place the other rectangle over the top of the jam. Use a fork to crimp and seal the edges all around the toaster pastry bite so that the jam stays inside. Repeat with the remaining pairs of rectangles.

5. Place the toaster pastry bites on the prepared baking sheet and lightly brush the tops and sides of each bite with the melted butter. Cut a tiny slit, about ⅛ inch (3 mm) long, in the top of each bite.

6. Bake for 10 minutes, or until golden brown. Let cool completely on the pan.

7. **To make the icing:** In a small bowl, whisk together the powdered sugar and milk until smooth and of spreading consistency.

8. Spread the icing on top of each cooled toaster pastry bite, leaving the crimped edges showing. Immediately sprinkle with the nonpareils.

Note

These bites can be made in advance and stored in an airtight container up to 3 days at room temperature or up to 5 days in the refrigerator. Enjoy at room temperature.

Apple Fritter Bites

These bites are crispy on the outside, fluffy on the inside, and have apple delight in every bite! Apple fritters are a fall favorite, and this version is baked, not fried, and so easy to make.

Apple Fritters

Nonstick cooking spray, for greasing

1½ cups (190 g) all-purpose flour

2 teaspoons baking powder

½ teaspoon kosher salt

2 teaspoons ground cinnamon

¼ cup (½ stick, or 55 g) unsalted butter, melted and slightly cooled

¼ cup (50 g) granulated sugar

1 large egg

½ teaspoon vanilla extract

½ cup (125 g) no-sugar-added applesauce

1½ cups (270 g) peeled and finely diced Honeycrisp apples (about 2 medium apples)

Glaze

2 cups (250 g) powdered sugar

⅓ cup plus 2 tablespoons (105 ml) apple cider or apple juice

1. **To make the apple fritters:** Preheat the oven to 400°F (200°C; gas mark 6). Spray a baking sheet with cooking spray.

2. In a medium bowl, whisk together the flour, baking powder, salt, and cinnamon until well combined.

3. Add the melted butter to a large bowl, then whisk in the sugar followed by the egg. Once combined, stir in the vanilla and applesauce. Add the flour mixture and stir until well combined, then fold in the chopped apples.

4. Scoop 1 tablespoon of batter into mounds a few inches (7.5 cm) apart on the prepared baking sheet. Bake for 10 minutes, then remove the fritters from the oven. Turn the broiler on high.

5. **Meanwhile, make the glaze:** In a small bowl, whisk together all the glaze ingredients. The glaze should be thin.

6. Brush some of the glaze over each fritter and let it drip down the sides. Return the fritters to the oven and broil for 2 to 4 minutes, until the glaze starts to caramelize the tops. Rotate the baking sheet every minute to ensure even caramelization. Be sure to carefully watch the fritters so they do not blacken and burn.

7. Brush the remaining glaze evenly over the broiled fritters. Let set on the baking sheet until the glaze hardens, about 15 minutes.

Note

These bites can be made in advance and stored in an airtight container for up to 2 days at room temperature or up to 1 week in the refrigerator. Enjoy at room temperature or reheat in the oven at 350°F (180°C; gas mark 4) for 5 to 10 minutes or in the microwave for 15 to 20 seconds.

Smoked Salmon Bagel Bites

MAKES

24

BITES

Carbs don't count when they're served as bites, right?! Fresh and bursting with flavor, these bagel bites are a simple, stunning, and scrumptious addition to any brunch or breakfast gathering. The classic combination of cream cheese, smoky salmon, crisp red onion, briny capers, cool cucumbers, and fresh dill makes for a super-satisfying bite.

Smoked Salmon Bagel Bites

3 mini plain bagels, cut in half

⅓ cup (75 g) whipped herb cream cheese

½ small red onion, cut into 24 thin rounds

1 package (8 ounces, or 227 g) smoked salmon, cut into 24 thin slices

2 cocktail cucumbers, cut into 24 thin rounds

24 large capers

Zest or juice of 1 lemon

1 tablespoon black and white sesame seeds, for garnishing

24 small sprigs fresh dill, for garnishing

Supplies

24 decorative food picks

1. Preheat the oven to 400°F (200°C; gas mark 6).

2. Lay the bagel halves, cut sides up, in a single layer on a baking sheet. Toast in the oven for 5 minutes, or until golden brown. Let cool slightly.

3. Spread each bagel half with a thick layer of cream cheese, then cut each half into quarters for 24 pieces total.

4. Top each bagel piece with a red onion round, a slice of smoked salmon, and a cucumber round. Place a caper on a food pick, then press the food pick down into the center of the cucumber all the way through the toasted bagel to hold everything together.

5. Sprinkle each bite with lemon zest or juice and the sesame seeds and finish with a sprig of dill.

Note

These bites can be assembled a day in advance. Cover loosely with plastic wrap and store in the refrigerator.

Blueberry Streusel, Muffin-Top Bites

MAKES
40
BITES

Top o' the mornin' to ya! Everyone prefers the muffin top, so let's bake it straight to the top. Filled with fresh blueberries and covered in a crunchy streusel, these bites are toasty on the outside, soft on the inside, and full of flavor.

Streusel Topping

¼ cup (½ stick, or 55 g) unsalted butter, melted and slightly cooled

¼ cup (50 g) granulated sugar

¼ cup (55 g) packed light brown sugar

¼ cup (30 g) all-purpose flour

Muffin Tops

1½ cups (190 g) all-purpose flour

2 teaspoons baking powder

½ teaspoon kosher salt

3 tablespoons unsalted butter, melted and slightly cooled

½ cup (100 g) granulated sugar

1 large egg

½ teaspoon vanilla extract

½ cup (120 ml) milk

1 cup (145 g) fresh blueberries

1. **To make the streusel topping:** In a small bowl, combine the ¼ cup (55 g) melted butter, ¼ cup (50 g) granulated sugar, brown sugar, and ¼ cup (30 g) flour with a fork until a crumbly mixture forms.

2. **To make the muffin tops:** Preheat the oven to 350°F (180°C; gas mark 4). Line a baking sheet with parchment paper.

3. In a medium bowl, whisk together the 1½ cups (190 g) flour, baking powder, and salt.

4. Add the 3 tablespoons melted butter to a large bowl, then whisk in the ½ cup (100 g) granulated sugar followed by the egg and vanilla until well combined. Whisk in the milk, then stir in the flour mixture until well combined. Gently fold in the blueberries.

5. Scoop 1 tablespoon of batter into mounds a few inches (7.5 cm) apart on the prepared baking sheet. Completely cover each mound with streusel, gently pressing it into the top and all over.

6. Bake for about 15 minutes, or until the muffin tops are golden brown and the streusel is crisp.

Note

These bites can be made in advance and stored in an airtight container up to 3 days at room temperature or up to 5 days in the refrigerator. Enjoy at room temperature or reheat in the oven at 350°F (180°C; gas mark 4) for about 5 minutes or in the microwave for 15 seconds each.

Avocado Toast Bites

There's no controversy that you'll love these bites! They're almost too easy to serve, and that's why your guests will go wild for them. They have double the avocado—mashed and sliced—and just enough egg to satisfy the full avo-toast experience. Don't rule them out for lunch or snack time.

Avocado Toast Bites

1 baguette (8 ounces, or 227 g)

3 small avocados, peeled and pitted, divided

1 to 2 tablespoons fresh lime juice (from 1 small lime)

Kosher salt, to taste

6 hard-boiled eggs, peeled

Garnishes

Flaky sea salt

Everything bagel seasoning

Crushed red pepper flakes (optional)

¼ cup (10 g) chopped fresh cilantro

1. Preheat the oven to 400°F (200°C; gas mark 6).

2. Slice the baguette into 24 thin slices and arrange on a baking sheet. Bake in the oven for 5 minutes, or until toasted and starting to turn golden brown.

3. Meanwhile, in a medium bowl, mash 1 avocado, then season with the fresh lime juice and kosher salt.

4. Slice the remaining 2 avocados into 24 thin slices.

5. Slice each hard-boiled egg into 4 round slices so that the white and yolk are intact.

6. Spread 1 teaspoon of mashed avocado onto each toasted slice of baguette, then top with a slice of avocado and a slice of hard-boiled egg.

7. Garnish with a sprinkle of sea salt, everything bagel seasoning, and red pepper flakes (if using). Finish with a sprinkle of chopped cilantro.

Note

These bites can be prepped a few hours in advance. Top the toast with the mashed and sliced avocado and brush with fresh lime juice to prevent the avocado from browning, then top with the hard-boiled egg slice. Cover loosely with plastic wrap and store in the refrigerator. Add the garnishes right before serving.

Chocolate Hazelnut Babka Bites

This bite-size take on the sweet, braided bread is chock-full of chocolate goodness! And it's not a labor of love, like classic babka is, as it is easily made with store-bought dough, chocolate hazelnut spread, and chocolate chips.

Flour, for dusting (optional)

1 can (8 ounces, or 227 g) refrigerated crescent rolls (8 count)

⅓ cup (80 g) chocolate hazelnut spread

¼ cup (45 g) mini chocolate chips, plus 2 tablespoons for sprinkling

1. Preheat the oven to 350°F (180°C; gas mark 4). Line a baking sheet with parchment paper.

2. On a lightly floured or parchment-lined work surface, roll out the crescent dough so that the perforated lines blend together and it measures about 15 x 8 inches (38 x 20 cm).

3. Spread the dough with the chocolate hazelnut spread, then sprinkle evenly with the mini chocolate chips.

4. Starting with a long end of the dough sheet, tightly roll up the dough into a log. With the seam side down, cut the log into 2½-inch (6 cm) sections so that you have 6 smaller logs. Cut each of these logs in half lengthwise, then turn each half so that the layers are facedown on the work surface. Cut each section in half lengthwise again for 24 pieces total.

5. Stretch each piece to about 4 inches (10 cm) and tie into a small knot. Place on the prepared baking sheet about 1 inch (2.5 cm) apart.

6. Bake for about 15 minutes, or until the babkas start to crisp and turn golden brown on top.

Note

These bites can be made up to 3 days in advance. Store in an airtight container at room temperature. Enjoy at room temperature or reheat in the oven at at 350°F (180°C; gas mark 4) for about 5 minutes or in the microwave for 15 seconds each.

Snack Bites

Got the munchies?! These brilliant bites are fun twists on everyday snacks that will change the way you nibble between meals and are also great for get-togethers. From a batch of After-School Snack Balls, loaded with peanut butter, pretzels, and cereals, to Bacon Mac 'n' Cheese Jalapeño Bites that will have everyone cheering for more during the big game, to Bean & Cheese Burrito Bites that could double as dinner (a.k.a. snack dinner!), these fun bites will keep hunger pangs at bay.

Bacon Mac 'n' Cheese Jalapeño Bites

MAKES
30
BITES

Win big with these bites! They're perfect for game day, potlucks, or any celebration you're wanting to spice up a bit. They can be prepped in advance and then just tossed in the oven shortly before the party for an easy-peasy-cheesy crowd-pleaser!

Nonstick cooking spray, for greasing

15 small jalapeños

1 cup (100 g) elbow macaroni

2 tablespoons unsalted butter

1 tablespoon all-purpose flour

1 teaspoon kosher salt

¼ teaspoon ground black pepper

1 cup (250 ml) milk

2 cups (230 g) shredded Cheddar, divided

8 slices bacon, cooked crisp and crumbled (about ¾ cup, or 165 g, bacon crumbles)

1. Preheat the oven to 350°F (180°C; gas mark 4). Line a baking sheet with parchment paper or foil and spray with nonstick cooking spray.

2. Cut each jalapeño in half lengthwise, leaving the stem intact, and remove the seeds. Slice a small sliver off the back of each half so that the jalapeños sit flat on the baking sheet, being careful not to slice all the way through. Place the jalapeño halves, cut sides up, on the prepared baking sheet.

3. In a medium pot, cook the macaroni to al dente according to the package directions. Drain.

4. Using the same pot, melt the butter over medium heat until it starts to sizzle. Add the flour, salt, and pepper and whisk until smooth, about 5 minutes. Slowly pour in the milk and whisk continuously. Continue to whisk occasionally until the mixture starts to thicken, about 3 minutes. Add 1½ cups (170 g) of the shredded Cheddar and stir until melted. Remove from the heat.

5. Add the cooked macaroni to the cheese sauce and stir to coat evenly. Stir in ⅓ cup (70 g) of the crumbled bacon. Let set for 5 minutes to cool and thicken slightly.

6. Fill each jalapeño half with mac 'n' cheese and sprinkle with the remaining cheese and bacon.

7. Bake for about 20 minutes, or until the jalapeños are soft and the cheese starts to turn golden brown on top.

8. Serve immediately, or keep warm in a 200°F (95°C; gas mark ¼) oven until ready to serve.

Note

These bites can be prepped a day in advance through step 6 to the point of baking. Store in an airtight container in the refrigerator, then proceed with steps 7 and 8.

BLT Grilled Cheese Bites

MAKES
24
BITES

Two popular sandwiches come together in these bites for the ultimate snack food! You won't be able to resist the layers of gooey grilled cheese topped with a special sauce, bacon, lettuce, and tomato. They are perfect for a picnic, a party, or just to satisfy a craving.

Special Sauce

½ cup (120 ml) mayonnaise

1 tablespoon bread-and-butter pickle juice

1 tablespoon Dijon mustard

1 tablespoon honey

1 teaspoon smoked paprika

1 teaspoon onion powder

1 teaspoon garlic powder

½ teaspoon kosher salt

½ teaspoon ground black pepper

BLT Grilled Cheese Sandwiches

6 slices bacon, for topping

¼ cup (½ stick, or 55 g) unsalted butter, softened, divided

8 slices soft white bread

6 slices deluxe American cheese (1½ slices per sandwich)

24 leaves butter leaf lettuce, for topping

8 cherry tomatoes, sliced into 3 thin slices crosswise, for topping

Supplies

24 decorative food picks

1. **To make the special sauce:** In a medium bowl, whisk together all the sauce ingredients until well combined.

2. **To make the BLT grilled cheese sandwiches:** Cook the bacon so that it is crispy yet still soft enough to fit easily onto a food pick without breaking. Cut each slice of cooked bacon into 4 pieces that are about 1½ inches (4 cm) long.

3. Spread some butter on one side of each slice of bread. Heat a large griddle or skillet over medium-low heat. Add 1 teaspoon of butter to the skillet and let melt. Place a slice of bread, buttered side down, over the melted butter and top with 1½ slices of cheese and another slice of bread, buttered side up. Cook for 4 to 5 minutes on each side, until the cheese melts and the bread is golden brown on the outside. Remove from the pan and let the sandwich set for a few minutes before cutting it into 6 pieces that are about 1½ inches (4 cm) square. Repeat with the remaining butter, bread slices, and cheese slices.

4. **To assemble:** Place ½ teaspoon of special sauce on top of each grilled cheese bite then add a piece of bacon, a folded leaf of lettuce, and a slice of cherry tomato. Press a food pick down into the center of the tomato slice all the way through the grilled cheese to hold everything together.

5. Serve immediately with the remaining special sauce, or keep warm in a 200°F (95°C; gas mark ¼) oven until ready to serve.

Deep-Dish Pizza Bites

No need for delivery with these yummy pizza bites! They're quick and easy to make for a trusty snack that will keep everyone pleased throughout a party or until dinner hits the table. You can also mix them up with different toppings.

Nonstick cooking spray, for greasing

4 burrito-size flour tortillas (10 inches, or 25 cm)

½ cup (120 ml) pizza sauce, plus more for serving

1½ cups (165 g) shredded mozzarella

1 cup (145 g) mini pepperoni or chopped pepperoni

1 tablespoon grated Parmesan

1 teaspoon dried Italian seasoning

¼ teaspoon garlic salt

1. Preheat the oven to 400°F (200°C; gas mark 6). Spray two 12-cup standard muffin pans with nonstick cooking spray.

2. Using a 3-inch (7.5 cm) round biscuit or cookie cutter, cut 6 rounds out of each tortilla for 24 tortilla rounds total. Press each tortilla round into a prepared muffin cup.

3. Spread 1 teaspoon of pizza sauce onto each tortilla round and top with 1 tablespoon shredded mozzarella cheese. Arrange 5 mini pepperoni or pepperoni pieces on top of the cheese.

4. Bake for 10 to 12 minutes, until the cheese bubbles and starts to turn golden brown in spots. Let cool in the pan for about 5 minutes.

5. Meanwhile, in a small bowl, whisk together the grated Parmesan, Italian seasoning, and garlic salt.

6. Transfer the pizza bites to a platter and sprinkle with the Parmesan seasoning mixture. Serve with more pizza sauce for topping or dipping.

Note

These bites can be prepped a day in advance through step 3 to the point of baking. Cover with plastic wrap and immediately refrigerate, then proceed with steps 4 through 6. They will need to bake for about 3 minutes longer because they will be cold coming straight from the refrigerator.

Popcorn Bites

Lights, TV, SNACKtion! Perfect for a movie night, these bites will be the stars of the show. They satisfy all the movie munchies with popcorn, peanuts, pretzels, and candy. They're gooey, sweet, salty, and totally delicious. Enjoy the show!

★

½ cup (1 stick, or 115 g) unsalted butter, plus more for greasing hands

1 bag (10 ounces, or 283 g) mini marshmallows

1 teaspoon vanilla extract

7 cups (56 g) popped salted popcorn

1 cup (120 g) broken thin pretzel sticks

¼ cup (40 g) roasted salted peanuts

½ cup (80 g) Milk Chocolate M&M'S Minis

¼ cup (45 g) mini chocolate chips

1. Add the butter and marshmallows to a large microwave-safe bowl. Microwave in 30-second intervals, stirring between each interval, until completely melted. Remove and stir in the vanilla until well combined.

2. Add the popcorn, pretzels, and peanuts to the marshmallow mixture and stir until well coated.

3. Let set until the mixture is cool enough to handle, then gently stir in the M&M'S Minis and chocolate chips.

4. Use buttered hands to form the mixture into twenty-four 2 tablespoon–size balls. Let set for at least 30 minutes to cool completely and become firm before serving.

Note

These bites can be made up to 2 days in advance. Store in an airtight container at room temperature.

Bean & Cheese Burrito Bites

MAKES
24
BITES

These burrito bites are simple, familiar, and delicious! All you need are five ingredients and less than thirty minutes to make a batch that will get gobbled up with glee. They're also great for freezing and reheating when you need a quick snack on the go.

Bean & Cheese Burrito Bites

½ cup (130 g) refried beans

½ cup (55 g) shredded Cheddar

1 tablespoon taco seasoning

6 burrito-size flour tortillas (10 inches, or 25 cm)

¼ cup (½ stick, or 55 g) unsalted butter, melted, divided

For Serving

Sour cream

Guacamole

Salsa

1. Preheat the oven to 400°F (200°C; gas mark 6). Line a baking sheet with parchment paper.

2. In a medium bowl, stir together the beans, shredded Cheddar, and taco seasoning until well combined.

3. Cut each flour tortilla into 4 wedges using a pizza slicer or sharp knife. You should have 24 wedges total. Heat the tortillas for 10 to 15 seconds in the microwave to make them easier to fold. Cover and keep warm while you prepare each burrito bite.

4. To assemble, spoon a heaping teaspoon of the bean and cheese mixture onto the wider half of a tortilla wedge. Fold in both sides, then roll up the tortilla like a burrito from the wide end to the pointed end. Brush some of the melted butter on the pointed end of the burrito to help seal it. Place the burrito bite, seam side down, on the prepared baking sheet. Repeat with the remaining tortillas and filling.

5. Brush the tops and sides of the burritos with the remaining melted butter. Bake for 10 to 12 minutes, until slightly crisp and starting to turn golden brown in spots.

6. Serve with sour cream, guacamole, and salsa for topping.

Note

These bites can be prepped up to 2 days in advance through step 4. Store in an airtight container in the refrigerator, then proceed with steps 5 and 6.

After-School Snack Balls

These hearty sweet-and-salty bites will have the kids rushing home from school for a snack before settling in to do their homework! Loaded with peanut butter, pretzels, cereal, dried cranberries, and chocolate, they're oh-so satisfying. And, if you need an after-school activity, let the kids have fun making these.

1 cup (25 g) toasted oat cereal (such as Cheerios)

1 cup (30 g) crisp rice cereal (such as Rice Krispies)

1 cup (95 g) mini pretzels or broken pretzel pieces

1 cup (85 g) quick oats

¾ cup (170 g) creamy peanut butter

¼ cup (60 ml) honey

⅓ cup (45 g) dried cranberries

⅓ cup (60 g) chocolate chips

1. In the bowl of a stand mixer fitted with the paddle attachment, mix the cereals, pretzels, quick oats, peanut butter, and honey on low speed until just combined. (You can also use a hand mixer.)

2. Add the dried cranberries and chocolate chips and mix until evenly distributed throughout.

3. Scoop the mixture into twenty-four 2 tablespoon–size portions. Using clean hands, form the portions into balls.

Note
These bites can be made up to 1 week in advance. Store in an airtight container at room temperature.

Loaded Baked Potato Chips

MAKES
24
BITES

These bites, dare I say, taste even better than loaded baked potatoes! The potato chips are baked with cheese and crispy bacon and then topped with sour cream and green onions. They're sure to get rave reviews from anyone who can get their hands on them.

24 whole wavy potato chips

1 cup (115 g) shredded Cheddar

⅓ cup (70 g) real bacon bits, divided

¼ cup (60 ml) sour cream

¼ cup (20 g) chopped green onion (about 3 green onions), for garnishing

1. Preheat the oven to 400°F (200°C; gas mark 6). Line a baking sheet with parchment paper.

2. Lay the potato chips in a single layer on the prepared baking sheet and top each one with about 2 teaspoons of shredded cheese and ½ teaspoon of bacon bits.

3. Bake for 5 minutes, or until the cheese melts.

4. Top each chip with ½ teaspoon of sour cream and a pinch each of the remaining bacon bits and green onion and serve.

Frito Chili Pie Bites

This is a fun way to serve this favorite southwestern dish! These Frito chips filled with flavorful chili and topped with melted cheese, chopped onion, and a dollop of pickled jalapeño cream sauce are perfect for any snacking scenario.

Frito Chili Pie Bites

1 tablespoon olive oil

1 medium white onion, chopped, divided

1 pound (454 g) ground beef

2 tablespoons chili powder

2 teaspoons dark brown sugar

1 teaspoon garlic powder

1 teaspoon ground cumin

1 teaspoon kosher salt

¼ cup (60 ml) beef broth

1 can (6 ounces, or 170 g) tomato paste

75 whole Fritos Scoops! (from a 9¼-ounce, or 262-g, bag)

2 cups (230 g) shredded Cheddar

Pickled Jalapeño Cream Sauce

¾ cup (180 ml) sour cream

¼ cup (22 g) finely chopped hot-and-sweet pickled jalapeños

1 tablespoon hot-and-sweet pickled jalapeño juice

1. **To make the Frito chili pie bites:** In a large pot, heat the olive oil over medium-high heat. Add half of the chopped onion and cook, stirring occasionally, until softened, about 5 minutes. Add the ground beef to the pot. Cook for 6 to 8 minutes, until the beef is browned, stirring occasionally with a wooden spoon to break it up into pieces. Drain off any grease, then add the chili powder, brown sugar, garlic powder, cumin, and salt and stir until well combined. Add the broth and tomato paste. Stir well, then remove from the heat.

2. Preheat the oven to 350°F (180°C; gas mark 4). Line a baking sheet with parchment paper.

3. Arrange the Fritos in a single layer on the prepared baking sheet with the scooped side facing up. Fill each one with the chili mixture, about 1 heaping teaspoon of chili, give or take. Top with a sprinkle of shredded cheese.

4. Bake for about 5 minutes, or until the cheese is just melted.

5. **Meanwhile, make the pickled jalapeño cream sauce:** In a small bowl, stir together all the sauce ingredients until well combined.

6. Top the bites with the remaining chopped onion and a dollop of the pickled jalapeño cream sauce. Serve with the remaining pickled jalapeño cream sauce on the side.

Note

The chili and pickled jalapeño cream sauce can be made up to 3 days in advance. Store separately in airtight containers in the refrigerator until ready to assemble, bake, and top the bites.

Fro-Yo Bites

Save yourself a trip to the frozen yogurt shop with these fun and customizable bites! Let the kids get creative with the toppings to make snack time extra tasty. These are so easy to make; I like to keep them stocked in the freezer for a cool snack that all the kids enjoy.

Fro-Yo Bites

1 cup (90 g) oats and honey granola, plus more for serving

¼ cup (55 g) creamy peanut or almond butter

Nonstick cooking spray, for greasing (optional)

1 cup (240 ml) vanilla Greek yogurt (full-fat will be the creamiest)

Toppings

Small blueberries

Chopped strawberries

Halved raspberries

Rainbow sprinkles

Mini chocolate chips

1. In a medium bowl, stir together the granola and nut butter until well combined, breaking up any large granola chunks as you mix.

2. Spray a 24-cup mini muffin pan with nonstick cooking spray or line with baking cups.

3. Fill the bottom of each prepared muffin cup with the granola mixture, about 1 teaspoon per cup. Top the granola with about 2 teaspoons of yogurt, filling each cup almost full.

4. Top the yogurt with fresh berries, sprinkles, chocolate chips, and/or more granola. Place in the freezer for at least 3 hours, or until firm.

5. To remove the bites from the pan, run a sharp knife around the edges to pop them out or turn the pan upside down on a clean surface and tap the bottom until they release. If you used baking cups, just pull up on the cups to remove them from the pan.

6. Let set at room temperature for 5 minutes to soften a bit before serving.

Note

These bites can be made up to 2 months in advance. Store in an airtight container in the freezer.

Monte Cristo Cracker Bites

These sweet-and-savory crackers will be the easiest and most desirable snack bites in your entertaining repertoire! They have all the familiar flavors of a traditional Monte Cristo sandwich and more—the crunch of the crackers; the savoriness of the ham, turkey, and cheese; the slight tang of the Dijon mustard; and the sweetness of the powdered sugar and raspberry jam.

Nonstick cooking spray, for greasing (optional)

¼ cup (½ stick, or 55 g) unsalted butter, melted and slightly cooled

1 tablespoon Dijon mustard

48 round crackers, divided

24 thinly shaved slices deli turkey breast

24 thinly shaved slices deli ham

12 ultra-thin slices Swiss cheese, cut in half

Powdered sugar, for dusting

Raspberry jam, for serving

1. Preheat the oven to 350°F (180°C; gas mark 4). Line a baking sheet with parchment paper or spray with nonstick cooking spray.

2. Add the melted butter to a small bowl, then stir in the Dijon until smooth.

3. Spread the bottoms of 24 crackers with the butter mixture and place them, buttered sides up, on the prepared baking sheet.

4. Top each cracker with a folded slice of turkey, a folded slice of ham, and a folded half slice of cheese.

5. Spread the tops of the remaining 24 crackers with the remaining butter mixture and place them, buttered sides up, on the bites.

6. Bake for 5 to 7 minutes, until the cheese is just melted and the tops of the crackers start to turn golden brown.

7. Dust the tops of the bites with powdered sugar and serve with raspberry jam for dipping.

Buffalo Chicken Celery Bites

MAKES
32
BITES

Make no bones about it, these bites are hard to beat! Baked boneless buffalo wings topped with a sliver of celery and crumbles of blue cheese let you enjoy all the deliciousness of chicken wings without the messy fingers. This snack is sure to satisfy whether you're watching the big game or hosting a houseful of hungry teens.

Buffalo Chicken Celery Bites

Nonstick cooking spray, for greasing

2 tablespoons unsalted butter, melted

¼ cup (60 ml) hot sauce, plus more for serving

1 pound (454 g) boneless, skinless chicken breasts, cut into 1- to 1½-inch (2.5 to 4 cm) pieces

½ cup (65 g) all-purpose flour

1 teaspoon garlic salt

1 teaspoon paprika

3 stalks celery, cut into ½-inch (1 cm) pieces

¼ cup (30 g) blue cheese crumbles

Blue cheese dressing, for serving

Supplies

32 decorative food picks

1. Preheat the oven to 425°F (220°C; gas mark 7). Line a rimmed baking sheet with foil. Set a wire baking rack on the baking sheet and coat the rack with cooking spray.

2. Add the melted butter to a medium bowl, then whisk in the hot sauce. Add the chicken pieces and toss until well coated.

3. Place the flour, garlic salt, and paprika in a resealable plastic bag and shake to mix. Transfer the chicken pieces to the bag, seal, and toss until well coated with the flour mixture. Place the chicken pieces onto the prepared baking rack and spray with cooking spray.

4. Bake for about 15 minutes, or until the chicken is crispy on the outside and no longer pink in the center. Let cool for a few minutes on the rack.

5. To assemble, place a piece of celery and a cooked chicken piece on each food pick and sprinkle with blue cheese crumbles.

6. Serve with blue cheese dressing and more hot sauce for dipping.

Note

The chicken can be made up to 2 days in advance. Store in an airtight container in the refrigerator, then reheat on a greased baking sheet in the oven at 350°F (180°C; gas mark 4) until the chicken is crisp and heated through. Proceed with assembling the bites.

PB&J-Stuffed Dates

These bites are snackable and healthy! They taste like a cross between a peanut butter and jelly sandwich and a Snickers bar—sweet and salty with a little crunch and lots of chew. The best part is that they take just minutes to make and store great in the refrigerator.

24 whole dates

½ cup (115 g) crunchy peanut butter

2 tablespoons jelly of choice

2 tablespoons chopped dark chocolate

1 tablespoon flaky sea salt

1. Remove the pit from each date by cutting a small slit across the top from end to end, leaving the bottom of the date intact. Gently open the slit and pry out the seed.

2. Fill each date with about 1 teaspoon of peanut butter and top with ¼ teaspoon jelly.

3. Sprinkle the jelly with chopped chocolate and a pinch of sea salt.

4. Refrigerate for at least 30 to set, then serve cold or at room temperature.

Note

These bites can be made up to 1 week in advance. Store in an airtight container in the refrigerator, then enjoy cold or at room temperature.

Dessert Bites

Trust me, you'll want to save room for dessert! These brilliant bites are the sweet ending that every occasion deserves. No need for sharing, as your guests will get to enjoy the taste without the guilt. From creamy Banana Pudding Bites that will be the hit of any barbecue and gooey Salted Caramel Molten Chocolate Cake Bites that will wow your dinner crowd to the no-bake Peanut Butter Pie Bites that will have everyone asking for the recipe, you're sure to enjoy the sweet life when serving these bites.

Banana Split Bites

Everyone will go bananas over these fun bites that look and taste just like an adorable banana split! You won't have to worry about melting ice cream with this simple way to serve a decadent, sweet summer treat.

5 bananas

1 cup (175 g) chocolate chips

1 tablespoon canola oil

¼ cup (30 g) chopped peanuts

¼ cup (50 g) rainbow sprinkles

¼ cup (12 g) whipped cream

25 Maraschino cherries

1. Line a baking sheet with parchment paper.

2. Cut five 1-inch-thick (2.5 cm) slices from each banana, making sure they are flat on both sides, for 25 banana slices total. Place on the prepared baking sheet.

3. In a medium microwave-safe bowl, heat the chocolate chips and oil in 30-second intervals, stirring after each interval, until just melted.

4. Spoon a few teaspoons of the melted chocolate onto the top of each banana slice, letting it slowly drip down the sides as it sets. Immediately sprinkle with chopped peanuts and rainbow sprinkles, then top with a dollop of whipped cream and a cherry.

Notes

- Brush the banana slices with lemon juice to slow browning.

- These bites can be made up to 2 days in advance, but don't top with the whipped cream and cherries until ready to serve. Store in an airtight container in the refrigerator.

- If you want frozen banana split bites, freeze them in an airtight container after topping with nuts and sprinkles for at least 2 hours and up to 1 week. Eat straight from the freezer as is or top with whipped cream and a cherry first. The bananas will become mushy once they thaw, so they must be enjoyed while frozen.

Baklava Bites

MAKES
24
BITES

These blissful bites are easily made with puff pastry instead of phyllo dough for an effortless way to enjoy baklava! Loaded with crunchy nuts, cinnamon, and sweet honey, they make for an amazing dessert that's sure to satisfy everyone's sweet tooth.

2 cups (280 g) mixed nuts (such as pistachios, walnuts, and cashews)

Nonstick cooking spray, for greasing

2 tablespoons unsalted butter, melted

¾ cup (180 ml) honey, divided

1 teaspoon fresh lemon juice

1 teaspoon ground cinnamon

Pinch of kosher salt

1 frozen puff pastry sheet, thawed according to the package directions

1. Preheat the oven to 375°F (190°C; gas mark 5).

2. Arrange the nuts in a single layer on a baking sheet and toast in the oven until golden and fragrant, about 8 minutes. Let the toasted nuts cool completely, then chop.

3. Lightly grease a 24-cup mini muffin pan with nonstick cooking spray. Line a baking sheet with parchment paper.

4. In a medium bowl, stir together the chopped nuts, melted butter, ½ cup (120 ml) of the honey, the lemon juice, cinnamon, and salt until evenly combined.

5. Using a rolling pin, roll out the puff pastry into a 10 x 15-inch (25 x 38 cm) rectangle. Cut the rectangle into twenty-four 2½-inch (6 cm) squares.

6. Place a square of puff pastry into each prepared muffin cup, pressing gently on the bottoms and up the sides so that the corners point up. Fill each cup with ½ tablespoon of the nut mixture.

7. Bake for 15 minutes, or until the nuts are lightly toasted but not burned and the pastry is golden brown. Let cool for 5 minutes before transferring the bites from the pan to the prepared baking sheet.

8. Drizzle the tops of the bites with the remaining honey. Let the honey soak in while the bites cool completely, about 1 hour, before serving.

Note

These bites can be made in advance and stored in an airtight container for up to 3 days at room temperature or up to 1 week in the refrigerator. Enjoy at room temperature.

Chocolate Chip Cookie Cannoli Bites

MAKES
24
BITES

This scrumptious spin on a traditional Italian treat fills crispy chocolate chip cookies with classic cannoli cream! Finish with a roll in pistachios to add some crunch.

Filling

1 cup (245 g) whole-milk ricotta

½ cup (112 g) mascarpone

¼ cup (30 g) powdered sugar

½ cup (50 g) crushed pistachios, for garnishing

Cookies

½ cup (1 stick, or 115 g) unsalted butter

¼ cup (55 g) packed light brown sugar

¼ cup (50 g) granulated sugar

1 large egg

½ teaspoon vanilla extract

1 cup (125 g) all-purpose flour

½ teaspoon baking soda

½ teaspoon kosher salt

⅓ cup (60 g) mini chocolate chips, plus more for sprinkling

1. **To make the filling:** In the bowl of a stand mixer fitted with the paddle attachment, beat the ricotta and mascarpone on medium until smooth. (You can also use a hand mixer.) Add the powdered sugar and beat on medium until well combined. Cover with plastic wrap and refrigerate for at least 30 minutes.

2. **To make the cookies:** Preheat the oven to 400°F (200°C; gas mark 6). Line three baking sheets with parchment paper (or bake in batches).

3. In a clean bowl of the stand mixer fitted with the paddle attachment, beat the butter and both sugars on medium speed until well combined. (You can also beat by hand or use a hand mixer.) Add the egg and vanilla and beat on medium speed until well incorporated. Stir in the flour, baking soda, and salt, then fold in the chocolate chips. Cover the dough with plastic wrap and refrigerate for 30 minutes.

4. Scoop 48 heaping 1 teaspoon–size portions of cookie dough a few inches (7.5 cm) apart onto the prepared baking sheets. Sprinkle each scoop of cookie dough with some mini chocolate chips. Press down on each scoop of dough to flatten slightly. Bake the cookies for 6 to 7 minutes, until golden brown and starting to crisp around the edges. Let the cookies cool completely.

5. **To assemble:** Once the cookies are cooled, remove the cannoli filling from the refrigerator. Turn half of the cookies over and scoop 1 tablespoon of filling onto them. Place another cookie on top of the filling to create a little cannoli sandwich. Sprinkle some crushed pistachios around the filling of each cannoli bite.

6. Serve immediately, or cover loosely with plastic wrap and refrigerate for up to 1 hour until ready to serve.

Note

The filling can be prepped up to 3 days and the cookie dough up to 5 days in advance. Store separately in an airtight container in the refrigerator.

Crêpe Bites

These bites can make for a seductive dessert or luxurious breakfast treat! My family loves to enjoy these mini crêpes for what we call "breakfast dessert" after a savory morning dish. A simple thin pancake is spread with chocolate hazelnut spread and folded with fresh fruit for a sweet ending to any meal.

Crêpes

¼ cup (½ stick, or 55 g) unsalted butter, melted and slightly cooled

1 cup (125 g) all-purpose flour

1¼ cups (300 ml) milk

½ teaspoon vanilla extract

1 large egg

2 tablespoons granulated sugar

Powdered sugar, for dusting

Fillings

1 cup (280 g) chocolate hazelnut spread

10 strawberries, sliced into 40 rounds

2 small bananas, sliced into 40 rounds

Supplies

40 decorative food picks

1. **To make the crêpes:** Add the melted butter, flour, milk, vanilla, egg, and granulated sugar to a blender. Blend until completely smooth, about 1 minute.

2. Heat a large nonstick skillet over medium-low heat. Cooking in batches, scoop 1 tablespoon of batter onto the pan and spread into a thin 4-inch (10 cm) round. (If you can fit another crêpe in the pan, space them about 1 inch, or 2.5 cm, apart.) Cook for 1 to 2 minutes per side, until golden in places but not crisp. You want the crêpes to be cooked all the way through but soft and foldable.

3. **To assemble:** Spread a thin layer of chocolate hazelnut spread onto the top side of each crêpe, then fold in half. Pinch the half in the middle and slip a strawberry slice in one side and a banana slice in the other side. Fold the crêpe in half again and secure with a food pick.

4. Dust each bite with powdered sugar right before serving.

Note

The crêpes can be made up to 2 days in advance. Store in an airtight container in the refrigerator, then let them come to room temperature before assembling or microwave for about 15 seconds to make sure they're soft and foldable before assembling.

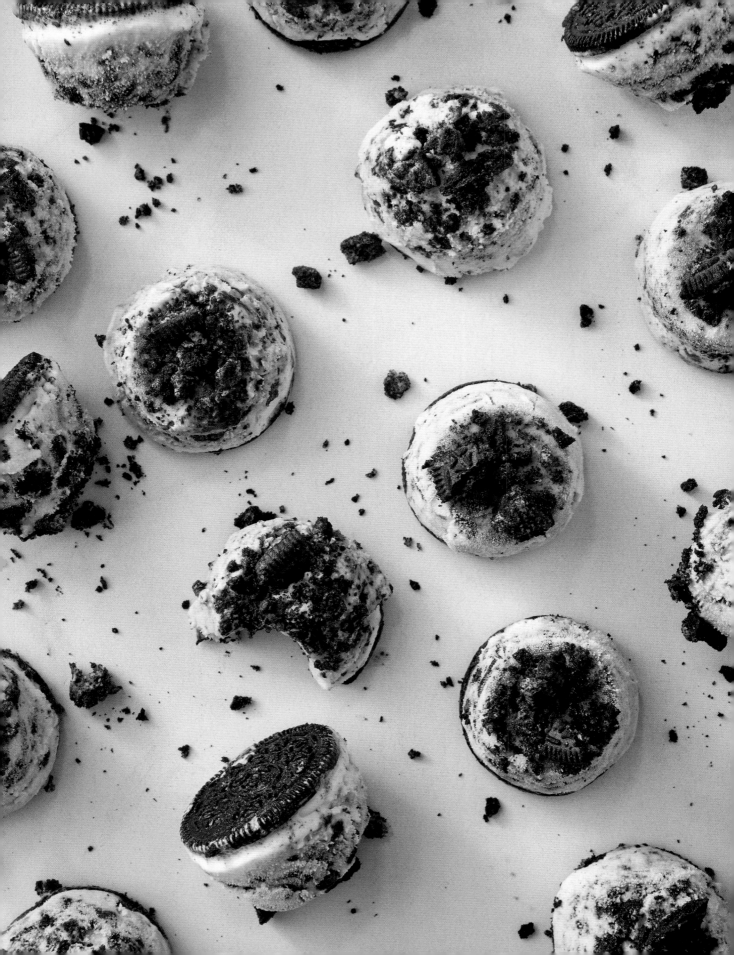

Cookies 'n' Cream Ice Cream Bites

MAKES
24
BITES

You'll create quite a storm of excitement with these bites! Just two ingredients and a little patience while they freeze is all it takes to stock your freezer with everyone's favorite creamy drive-thru treat, made playful and easy to pop in your mouth.

Nonstick cooking spray, for greasing

24 Oreo cookies

2 cups (300 g) vanilla ice cream, slightly softened

1. Spray a 24-cup mini muffin pan with nonstick cooking spray or line with baking cups.

2. Carefully separate all the Oreos, leaving the 24 halves with the creme whole and crushing the 24 creme-less halves.

3. In the bowl of a stand mixer fitted with the paddle attachment, beat the ice cream and half of the crushed Oreos on low speed until the ice cream is creamy and the cookie pieces are distributed throughout, about 1 minute. (You can also use a hand mixer.)

4. Fill each prepared muffin cup almost three-quarters full with the ice cream mixture (about 1 tablespoon per cup). Gently press an Oreo half, creme side down, on top of the ice cream in each muffin cup. Cover with plastic wrap and freeze for at least 4 hours.

5. Run a sharp knife around the edge of each bite to remove from the pan. Turn the bites out, cookie sides down, onto a parchment-lined baking sheet. Top each bite with the remaining crushed Oreos. Return to the freezer for at least 1 hour before serving.

Note

These bites can be made up to 1 month in advance. Store in an airtight container in the freezer.

Apple Pie Bites

These bites are baked to *pie*-fection for a quick pie lover's fix! Strips of piecrust are simply wrapped around apple slices and flavored with lots of cinnamon and sugar. Be sure to serve with the caramel sauce to elevate the enjoyment.

¼ cup (50 g) granulated sugar

2 teaspoons ground cinnamon

1 large or 2 medium Honeycrisp apples

Flour, for dusting

1 refrigerated piecrust (9 inches, or 23 cm)

3 tablespoons unsalted butter, melted, divided

Caramel sauce, for dipping

1. Preheat the oven to 400°F (200°C; gas mark 6). Line a baking sheet with parchment paper.

2. In a small bowl, whisk together the sugar and cinnamon.

3. Slice the apple(s) into twenty ¼-inch-thick (6 mm) slices and place them in a large bowl. Add 1 tablespoon of the cinnamon-sugar mixture and toss to coat the apples evenly.

4. On a lightly floured cutting board, using a rolling pin, roll out the piecrust dough to a 10-inch (25 cm) square. Brush with half of the melted butter, then sprinkle with half of the remaining cinnamon-sugar mixture, covering the dough completely.

5. Using a sharp knife or pizza cutter, cut the dough into twenty ½-inch-thick (1 cm) strips.

6. Wrap each apple slice loosely in a strip of the dough, with the cinnamon-sugar side of the dough touching the apple. Tuck in the ends of the dough strips and place on the prepared baking sheet. Brush the dough-wrapped apple slices all over with the remaining melted butter, then sprinkle with the remaining cinnamon-sugar mixture.

7. Bake for 15 minutes, or until the crust is golden brown.

8. Serve with caramel sauce for dipping.

Note

These bites can be made up to 3 days in advance. Store in an airtight container in the refrigerator. Enjoy at room temperature or reheat in the oven at 350°F (180°C; gas mark 4) for about 5 minutes.

Brookie Bites

MAKES
24
BITES

You can have your cookies . . . and brownies and eat them too! Chewy chocolate chip cookies and gooey brownies are baked together to create the ultimate way to enjoy two favorite desserts in one double-delicious bite—the dream team of treats.

Cookie Dough

Nonstick cooking spray, for greasing

¼ cup (½ stick, or 55 g) unsalted butter, softened

¼ cup (55 g) packed light brown sugar

2 tablespoons granulated sugar

1 large egg

½ teaspoon vanilla extract

½ cup (65 g) all-purpose flour

¼ teaspoon baking soda

⅛ teaspoon kosher salt

¼ cup (45 g) mini semisweet chocolate chips, plus 2 tablespoons for garnishing

Brownie Batter

¼ cup (½ stick, or 55 g) unsalted butter, melted and slightly cooled

½ cup (100 g) granulated sugar

1 large egg

½ teaspoon vanilla extract

½ cup (65 g) flour

2 tablespoons cocoa powder

¼ teaspoon baking powder

⅛ teaspoon kosher salt

1. Preheat the oven to 350°F (180°C; gas mark 4). Lightly grease a 24-cup mini muffin pan with nonstick cooking spray.

2. **To make the cookie dough:** In the bowl of a stand mixer fitted with the paddle attachment, beat the butter and both sugars on medium until well combined. (You can also beat by hand or with a hand mixer.) Add the egg and vanilla and beat on medium until well combined. Beat in the flour, baking soda, and salt on medium until well combined, then fold in the mini chocolate chips. Place in the refrigerator while you prepare the brownie batter.

3. **To make the brownie batter:** Add the melted butter to a medium bowl, then whisk in the granulated sugar until well combined. Whisk in the egg and vanilla, then stir in the flour, cocoa powder, baking powder, and salt until well incorporated.

4. Add 1 heaping teaspoon of cookie dough to one-half of each prepared muffin cup, then add 1 heaping teaspoon of brownie batter to the other half, filling each muffin cup about halfway full. Press some mini chocolate chips into the tops of the cookie dough halves.

5. Bake for about 10 minutes, or until the brownie batter and cookie dough are both set around the edges and the cookie dough is starting to turn golden brown on top. Let cool completely in the pan before serving. Use a spatula or sharp knife to help loosen the brookie bites from the pan.

Note

These bites can be made up to 5 days in advance. Store in an airtight container at room temperature.

Banana Pudding Bites

This comfort food classic in a bite is mmm-AZING! Great to serve as dessert at a barbecue, picnic, or any get-together, they can be prepped in a matter of minutes with four simple ingredients for easy enjoyment.

24 vanilla wafer cookies, plus crushed cookies for garnishing

3 bananas

¼ cup (60 g) vanilla pudding

¼ cup (12 g) whipped cream

1. Arrange the cookies in a single layer on a work surface or platter.

2. Cut the bananas into twenty-four ¼-inch-thick (6 mm) slices. Place a slice of banana on each cookie.

3. Top each slice of banana with ½ teaspoon each of pudding and whipped cream.

4. Garnish each bite with crushed wafer cookies.

5. Serve immediately, or cover loosely with plastic wrap and refrigerate for up to 2 hours until ready to serve.

Chocolate Cheesecake Strawberry Bites

MAKES

24

BITES

Simple and stylish, these bites will become your signature sweet treat for special occasions! They taste like chocolate-covered strawberries but are even tastier with the enhancement of creamy, no-bake chocolate cheesecake stuffed inside the juicy, sweet strawberry halves.

1 package (8 ounces, or 227 g) cream cheese, softened

1 cup (125 g) powdered sugar

1 teaspoon vanilla extract

½ cup (85 g) dark chocolate chips

12 large strawberries

¼ cup (45 g) mini chocolate chips, for garnishing

1. In the bowl of a stand mixer fitted with the paddle attachment, beat the cream cheese and powdered sugar on low speed, increasing to medium, until well combined. (You can also use a hand mixer.) Beat in the vanilla.

2. In a small microwave-safe bowl, heat the chocolate chips in 30-second intervals, stirring after each interval, until melted. Let cool slightly. Add the melted chocolate to the cream cheese mixture and beat on low speed until just combined, then on high speed until smooth. Cover and refrigerate for at least 30 minutes.

3. Meanwhile, wash and dry the strawberries. Slice each strawberry in half lengthwise through the stem, leaving the stem intact. Using a small spoon or strawberry huller, hollow out the middle of each strawberry half, being careful not to go too deep.

4. Place the chilled cheesecake mixture in a piping bag with a decorating tip or a resealable plastic bag with a corner snipped off, then pipe into each strawberry half. Garnish with the mini chocolate chips.

5. Store in the refrigerator until ready to serve. These are best served within 2 hours of filling the strawberries, but I recommend waiting to fill the strawberries until right before serving.

Salted Caramel Molten Chocolate Cake Bites

MAKES
24
BITES

These bites are bound to be love at first bite! Easy to make and with a gooey salted caramel surprise inside, these drool-worthy cakes are sure to impress your guests.

Nonstick cooking spray, for greasing

¼ cup (½ stick, or 55 g) unsalted butter

⅓ cup (60 g) semisweet chocolate chips

¼ cup (50 g) granulated sugar

¼ cup (30 g) powdered sugar

2 tablespoons heavy cream

½ teaspoon vanilla extract

¼ cup (30 g) all-purpose flour

2 large eggs

2 large egg yolks

24 ROLO candies

Flaky sea salt, for garnishing

1. Preheat the oven to 400°F (200°C; gas mark 6). Grease a 24-cup mini muffin pan with nonstick cooking spray and set on a rimmed baking sheet.

2. In a large microwave-safe bowl, heat the butter and chocolate chips in 30-second intervals, whisking after each interval, until melted, about 2 minutes. Add both sugars to the melted chocolate and whisk until well combined. Whisk in the heavy cream and vanilla. Add the flour and whisk until just combined.

3. In a separate large bowl, whisk the eggs and egg yolks with a handheld mixer on high speed until pale yellow and airy, about 5 minutes.

4. Using a rubber spatula, fold the egg mixture into the chocolate mixture until well blended. The batter will be thin and bubbly. Pour the batter into the prepared muffin cups, filling each one halfway full. Place a ROLO in the center of the batter in each cup.

5. Bake for 8 to 10 minutes, until set around the edges and starting to puff around the ROLO. Remove from the oven and immediately sprinkle each cake with a little sea salt. Let set for 10 minutes in the muffin pan before running a knife around the edges and removing each bite.

Note

These bites can be made up to 5 days in advance. Store in an airtight container in the refrigerator, then reheat in the microwave for 5 to 10 seconds each and serve immediately or at room temperature.

Coconut Key Lime Pie Bites

Take a trip to the tropics with these tantalizing treats! A coconutty graham cracker crust is topped with a refreshing key lime cream for a no-bake dessert that's the perfect balance of sweet and tangy.

Crust

⅓ cup (40 g) graham cracker crumbs

¼ cup (20 g) sweetened coconut flakes

2 tablespoons granulated sugar

3 tablespoons unsalted butter, melted

Filling

1 package (8 ounces, or 227 g) cream cheese, softened

½ cup (120 ml) coconut Greek yogurt

3 tablespoons fresh key lime juice plus 1 teaspoon zest, divided

½ cup (24 g) whipped cream

¼ cup (20 g) sweetened coconut flakes

Garnishes

Toasted sweetened coconut flakes (see Notes)

Whipped cream

2 teaspoons lime zest

24 thin lime wedges

1. **To make the crust:** Line a 24-cup mini muffin pan with baking cups.

2. Add the graham cracker crumbs, coconut flakes, and sugar to a medium bowl. Stir in the melted butter until well incorporated. Press 1 teaspoon of the crust mixture into the bottom of each prepared muffin cup.

3. **To make the filling:** In the bowl of a stand mixer fitted with the paddle attachment, beat the cream cheese and yogurt on medium speed until smooth, scraping down the sides and bottom of the bowl as needed. (You can also use a hand mixer.) Turn the mixer to low speed and slowly add the lime juice. Add the whipped cream and beat on low until well incorporated and smooth. Stir in the coconut flakes and lime zest.

4. Place about 2 teaspoons of the filling on top of each crust, filling each cup all the way full. Cover with plastic wrap and refrigerate for at least 4 hours before serving.

5. When ready to serve, top with toasted coconut, more whipped cream, a sprinkle of lime zest, and a lime wedge.

Notes

- Toasted coconut can be hard to find in stores, so here's how to toast it yourself: Preheat the oven to 350°F (180°C; gas mark 4). Spread the coconut flakes on a rimmed baking sheet and bake, stirring often, for about 5 minutes, or until golden brown and fragrant.

- These bites can be made up to 1 week in advance through step 4. Store in an airtight container in the refrigerator, then garnish with the toasted coconut, whipped cream, lime zest, and lime wedges before serving.

Strawberry Shortcake Bites

MAKES
30
BITES

All the goodness of strawberry shortcake is rolled into a super-easy, no-bake, melt-in-your-mouth bite! These bites are fun to serve for a special spring or summer gathering.

1 frozen pound cake (16 ounces, or 454 g), thawed

¼ cup (25 g) white cake frosting

1 cup (150 g) finely chopped fresh strawberries

1 package (16 ounces, or 454 g) vanilla candy coating

¼ cup (5 g) crushed dried strawberries, for garnishing

1. Line a baking sheet with parchment paper.

2. Crumble the thawed pound cake into the bowl of a stand mixer fitted with the paddle attachment, then add the frosting and beat on medium speed until the mixture starts to come together. (You can also use a hand mixer.) Add the chopped strawberries and beat on low speed until they are evenly distributed throughout the cake mixture.

3. Form the cake mixture into thirty heaping 1 tablespoon–size balls and place on the prepared baking sheet. Cover the pan loosely with plastic wrap and refrigerate for at least 1 hour or freeze for about 15 minutes to harden.

4. When ready to coat the cake balls, melt the candy coating according to the package directions. Line another baking sheet with parchment paper. Remove the cake balls from the refrigerator (or freezer) and coat them, one at a time, in the melted candy coating, using a fork to gently roll each cake ball in it. Try to keep some candy coating between the cake ball and the fork at all times to maintain a smooth coating and the round shape of the cake ball. Lift out carefully and let the excess candy coating drip off before placing on the prepared baking sheet.

5. Immediately sprinkle each coated cake bite with some crushed dried strawberries. Allow the cake bites to harden completely, then break off any excess candy coating that may have gathered around the bottom of the bites.

Note

These bites can be made up to 5 days in advance. Store in an airtight container in the refrigerator, then let sit, uncovered, for 10 minutes at room temperature before enjoying.

Peanut Butter Pie Bites

Be still all peanut-butter-loving hearts with this perfectly portioned pie! The salty peanut butter–filled pretzel crust paired with a sweet, creamy peanut butter filling makes for an abundance of peanut-butter delight in every bite.

Pretzel Crust

3 cups (288 g) peanut butter–filled pretzel nuggets (or plain pretzel nuggets)

½ cup (115 g) creamy peanut butter

¼ cup (60 ml) honey

Filling

½ cup (115 g) creamy peanut butter

½ package (4 ounces, or 113 g) cream cheese, softened

½ cup (65 g) powdered sugar

1½ cups (108 g) whipped topping

Garnish

12 peanut butter–filled pretzel nuggets, cut in half, or crushed pretzels

1. **To make the pretzel crust:** Add the pretzel nuggets to a food processor and blend into fine crumbs. Add the peanut butter and honey and blend until well incorporated.

2. Press 1 heaping tablespoon of the crust mixture into and up the sides of each cup of a nonstick 24-cup mini muffin pan (or spray with nonstick cooking spray if not a nonstick pan). Place in the freezer while you prepare the filling, or refrigerate for at least 1 hour.

3. **Meanwhile, make the filling:** In the bowl of a stand mixer fitted with the paddle attachment, beat the peanut butter and cream cheese on medium speed until smooth. (You can also use a hand mixer.) Add the powdered sugar and beat on low speed, increasing to medium, until well combined. Add the whipped topping and beat on low until just incorporated. Turn the mixer to medium-high and beat until smooth and creamy.

4. Fill each crust completely full with filling, about 1 tablespoon. Cover with plastic wrap and refrigerate for at least 4 hours before serving.

5. Run a knife around the edge of each bite to remove from the pan. When ready to serve, garnish with a pretzel nugget half or crushed pretzels.

Note

These bites can be made up to 3 days in advance. Store in an airtight container in the refrigerator, then enjoy cold.

Savvy Sips

Complete the occasion with a complementary cocktail that stands out for its sippable savviness. These are no standard sips, my friends—they're tasty twists on beloved classics, such as an old-fashioned with fig or a bee's knees with sage, as well as clever creations you'd never expect to enjoy so much, such as an Eggnog Bite or a Piña Colada Popsicle Shot. All are fun, flavorful, well balanced, and beautiful, and you can make most of them into mocktails by simply taking out the booze for thoughtful sips that everyone will enjoy and remember. Salute!

Espresso S'more-tini

MAKES

1

SIP

This is a decadent drink that makes for a fun summer night soiree! Each sweet sip of this s'more-inspired espresso martini will make you feel like you're fireside, where the marshmallows are roasting and the smells of chocolate and graham crackers soothe your senses.

Hot fudge or chocolate syrup, for the rim

Graham cracker crumbs, for the rim

Ice, for the cocktail shaker

2 ounces (60 ml) vodka

½ ounce (15 ml) coffee liqueur (such as Kahlúa)

1 ounce (30 ml) brewed espresso or coffee, cooled

½ ounce (15 ml) chocolate syrup

1 large marshmallow, for garnishing

1. Coat the rim of a martini glass with hot fudge or chocolate syrup, then dip the rim into graham cracker crumbs.

2. Fill a cocktail shaker with ice.

3. Add the vodka, coffee liqueur, cooled espresso, and chocolate syrup to the cocktail shaker and shake for 10 to 20 seconds, until well chilled.

4. Strain into the prepared martini glass.

5. Toast a marshmallow with a kitchen torch (or under the broiler), then place on top of the drink.

The Fashionable Fig

This delicious new take on an old-fashioned is infused with fig! With its beautiful balance and sippable smoothness, you'll be making this cocktail all year round.

Ice, for the glass and cocktail shaker

1 tablespoon fig jam

1 ounce (30 ml) fresh lemon juice

2 ounces (60 ml) bourbon

½ ounce (15 ml) Cointreau

1 ounce (30 ml) sparkling water

1 slice fresh fig, for garnishing (optional)

1. To a rocks glass, add a large ice cube that fits the glass or fill the glass three-quarters full with ice.

2. Add the fig jam and lemon juice to a cocktail shaker and stir until well incorporated.

3. Add the bourbon, Cointreau, and ice and shake until well chilled.

4. Double-strain into the rocks glass, add the sparkling water, and stir to incorporate.

5. Garnish with the fig slice (if using).

The Sage Bee

Everyone will be buzzing about this simple sage-infused cocktail! This take on the Prohibition-era bee's knees is sophisticated in its balance of beautiful flavors and is to *bee* love at first sip.

5 leaves fresh sage, plus 1 for garnish

¾ ounce (22.5 ml) honey syrup (mixture of equal amounts of honey and water)

2 ounces (60 ml) gin

¾ ounce (22.5 ml) fresh lemon juice

¼ ounce (7.5 ml) Yellow Chartreuse

Ice, for the cocktail shaker

1. Chill a coupe glass.

2. Add the 5 sage leaves and the honey syrup to a cocktail shaker and muddle.

3. Add the gin, lemon juice, Yellow Chartreuse, and ice and shake for 10 to 20 seconds, until well chilled.

4. Strain into the chilled coupe glass and garnish with the sage leaf.

rty Dill Martini

his is a surprisingly tasty twist on a classic martini! The addition of dill pickle juice gives this cocktail a deliciously dirty tang.

Ice, for the cocktail shaker

2 ounces (60 ml) vodka or gin (based on personal preference)

½ ounce (15 ml) dry vermouth

½ ounce (15 ml) dill pickle juice

1 cornichon, for garnishing

1 sprig fresh dill, for garnishing

1. Chill a coupe glass.

2. Fill a cocktail shaker with ice.

3. Add the vodka, vermouth, and pickle juice to a cocktail shaker and shake for 10 to 20 seconds, until well chilled.

4. Strain into the chilled coupe glass and garnish with the cornichon and sprig of dill.

Frozen Strawberry Lemonade Daquiri Swirl

MAKES

2

SIPS

This will be the drink of your summer—a swirly sip that's as pretty as it is pleasing! It's so easy to make each daiquiri flavor, then swirl them in the glass for optimal enjoyment.

Strawberry Daiquiri

2 ounces (60 ml) white rum

1 ounce (30 ml) fresh lime juice

½ ounce (15 ml) simple syrup

½ cup (75 g) fresh or frozen strawberries

½ cup ice

Lemonade Daiquiri

2 ounces (60 ml) white rum

1½ ounces (45 ml) fresh lemon juice

½ ounce (15 ml) limoncello

1 ounce (30 ml) simple syrup

1 cup ice

Garnishes

1 strawberry

1 lemon wedge

1. Prepare each flavor of daiquiri separately by adding all ingredients to a clean blender and blending until smooth.

2. Pour half of one flavor of frozen daiquiri into a small coupe or hurricane glass, then add half of the other frozen daiquiri, swirling as you pour. Use a cocktail stirrer to swirl a little more once both blended daiquiris are in the glass. Repeat in a second glass with the remaining daiquiris.

3. Garnish with the strawberry and lemon wedge.

Note

To turn this sip into a mocktail, leave out the rum and limoncello. Because of the reduced amount of liquid, it will make only one sip, not two.

Mango Mai Tai

Take me to the tiki bar with this cocktail! This classic drink is made with mango for a tropical fruity twist perfect for a poolside sip.

⅓ cup (50 g) mango chunks, plus 2 slices for garnishing

Ice, for the glass and cocktail shaker

2 ounces (60 ml) aged rum

½ ounce (15 ml) Cointreau or orange curaçao

¾ ounce (22.5 ml) fresh lime juice

½ ounce (15 ml) orgeat syrup

1 sprig fresh mint, for garnishing

1 Maraschino cherry, for garnishing

1. Add the mango chunks to a cocktail shaker and muddle until pureed.

2. Fill a rocks or highball glass three-quarters full with ice.

3. Add the rum, Cointreau, lime juice, orgeat, and ice to the shaker and shake for 10 to 20 seconds, until well chilled.

4. Double-strain into the prepared highball glass.

5. Garnish with the sprig of mint, mango slices, and cherry.

Orange Cream Mimosa

MAKES

1

SIP

This creamy sparkling sip is a must-have for your next breakfast or brunch get-together! It is easily crafted in minutes and tastes just like the favorite childhood treat but with a grown-up twist.

Ice, for the cocktail shaker

2 ounces (60 ml) orange juice

½ ounce (15 ml) Cointreau

½ ounce (15 ml) half-and-half

2 ounces (60 ml) champagne, prosecco, or sparkling white wine

Orange peel twist, for garnishing

1. Fill a cocktail shaker with ice.

2. Add the orange juice, Cointreau, and half-and-half to the cocktail shaker and shake for 10 to 20 seconds, until well chilled.

3. Strain into a champagne flute.

4. Top with the champagne and stir to combine.

5. Garnish with the orange twist.

Note

To turn this sip into a mocktail, leave out the Cointreau and replace the champagne with sparkling grape juice, sparkling water, or ginger ale or lemon-lime soda.

Piña Colada Popsicle Shots

If you like piña coladas, you're going to love these inventive Popsicle shots! Turn one of summer's favorite sips into a fun frozen shot that will take you and your friends to a tropical paradise as you enjoy them.

Popsicle Shots

1 cup (165 g) pineapple chunks (fresh or frozen)

4 ounces (120 ml) white rum

3 ounces (90 ml) cream of coconut

2 ounces (60 ml) coconut milk

1 ounce (30 ml) fresh lime juice

Garnishes

8 thin slivers fresh pineapple

8 small lime wedges

8 Maraschino cherries

Supplies

8 plastic shot cups (1½ ounces, or 45 ml)

8 cocktail umbrellas

1. In a blender, blend the pineapple chunks, rum, coconut cream, coconut milk, and lime juice until smooth.

2. Fill each shot cup with the blended drink, then freeze for 1 hour.

3. Remove and insert a cocktail umbrella into the center of each shot cup. Garnish with a sliver of fresh pineapple, a wedge of lime, and a cherry.

4. Return to the freezer for at least another hour, or until frozen completely.

5. When ready to serve, squeeze the Popsicles from the shot cups and serve immediately.

Notes

- These sips can be made up to 3 weeks in advance. Store in an airtight container in the freezer.

- To turn this sip into a mocktail, leave out the rum.

Verde Maria

Move over Bloody Mary, the Verde Maria is here to brighten up the brunch menu! A blend of fresh and zesty greens is combined with tequila for a flavorful and smooth sip that has a slight kick. Perfect for brunch, game day, Saint Patrick's Day, Cinco de Mayo, or any occasion where you want to serve a savory sip.

Verde Maria Mix (makes enough for 2 drinks)

1 small tomatillo, peeled and cut in half

½ medium green tomato

½ large rib celery, chopped

4 thick slices seedless cucumber

¼ cup (10 g) packed fresh cilantro leaves

1½ ounces (45 ml) fresh lime juice

1 ounce (30 ml) simple syrup

1 slice jalapeño, seeds removed and chopped

Cocktail

Ice, for the glass

6 ounces (180 ml) Verde Maria Mix

2 ounces (60 ml) blanco tequila

Garnishes

1 small rib celery

3 thin slices seedless cucumber, on a decorative cocktail pick

2 slices jalapeño, seeds removed, if desired

1 lime wedge, for serving

1. **To make the Verde Maria mix:** In a blender, blend the tomatillo, green tomato, celery, cucumber, cilantro, lime juice, simple syrup, and jalapeño until smooth.

2. **To make the cocktail:** Fill a rocks or highball glass three-quarters full with ice.

3. Add the Verde Maria mix and tequila to the prepared glass and stir briskly to combine and chill.

4. Garnish with the celery rib, cucumber skewer, and jalapeño slices and serve with the lime wedge.

Notes

- The Verde Maria mix can be made up to 2 days in advance. Store in an airtight container in the refrigerator, then just shake well until smooth before making the cocktail.

- To turn this sip into a mocktail, leave out the tequila and enjoy as a green juice or replace it with sparkling water.

Pumpkin Paloma

Elevate the traditional tequila cocktail with pumpkin and spice and everything nice for a refreshing fall drink! It's a bright and beautiful sip that complements the coziness of the season so well.

Ice, for the glass and cocktail shaker

2 ounces (60 ml) mezcal

1 ounce (30 ml) fresh grapefruit juice

½ ounce (15 ml) fresh lime juice

¼ ounce (7.5 ml) agave syrup

1 tablespoon canned 100% pure pumpkin

¼ teaspoon pumpkin pie spice, plus more for garnishing

1. Fill a highball glass three-quarters full with ice.

2. Fill a cocktail shaker with ice.

3. Add the mezcal, grapefruit juice, lime juice, agave, pumpkin, and pumpkin spice to the cocktail shaker and shake for 10 to 20 seconds, until well chilled.

4. Double-strain into the prepared highball glass.

5. Garnish with a dash of pumpkin pie spice.

Note

To turn this sip into a mocktail, replace the mezcal with sparkling water or lemon-lime soda.

Merry Margarita

MAKES
1
SIP

This seasonal sip is sure to add spirit to your holiday celebrations! The cranberry flavor gives a festive twist to the classic margarita. Simple and not too sweet, it's perfect for cheers-ing with friends all season long.

Sugared Cranberries

1½ cups (300 g) granulated sugar, divided

1 bag (16 ounces, or 454 g) whole fresh cranberries

Merry Margarita

1 sprig fresh rosemary, plus more for garnishing

6 fresh or frozen cranberries

1 teaspoon agave syrup

Ice, for the glass and cocktail shaker

2 ounces (60 ml) reposado tequila (blanco or añejo tequila also works)

½ ounce (15 ml) Cointreau (or other orange liqueur)

1 ounce (30 ml) cranberry juice

½ ounce (15 ml) fresh lime juice

3 sugared cranberries, for garnishing

1. **To make the sugared cranberries:** Place a wire rack on a rimmed baking sheet.

2. In a medium pot, combine ½ cup (100 g) of the sugar with ½ cup (120 ml) of water over medium heat, stirring until the sugar is dissolved, 2 to 3 minutes. Stir in the cranberries until completely coated.

3. Using a slotted spoon, transfer the cranberries to the prepared wire rack. Let them dry for at least 1 hour.

4. Place the remaining 1 cup (200 g) sugar in a shallow dish. Roll the cranberries around in the sugar until completely coated. Let dry for at least 1 hour before enjoying.

5. **To make the merry margarita:** Add the leaves from the sprig of rosemary, fresh or frozen cranberries, and agave to a cocktail shaker. Muddle the ingredients until the cranberries are smashed and all the ingredients are well incorporated.

6. Fill a rocks glass three-quarters full with ice.

7. Add the tequila, Cointreau, cranberry juice, lime juice, and ice to the cocktail shaker and shake for 10 to 20 seconds, until well chilled.

8. Double-strain into the prepared rocks glass.

9. Garnish with the sprig of rosemary and sugared cranberries.

Note

To turn this sip into a mocktail, replace the tequila and Cointreau with sparkling water or lemon-lime soda.

Eggnog Bites

It doesn't matter if this is a bite or a sip, because it's just delicious! A spiked eggnog cream is served in a spiced sugar cookie cup for an unforgettable holiday sip that doubles as a dessert.

Eggnog Filling

1 cup (250 ml) heavy cream

¾ cup (180 ml) eggnog

3 tablespoons spiced rum

1 tablespoon granulated sugar

Sugar Cookie Cups

Nonstick cooking spray, for greasing

2 tablespoons granulated sugar

2 tablespoons ground cinnamon

1 package (16 ounces, or 454 g) refrigerated ready-to-bake sugar cookie dough (24 count), slightly softened

Garnishes

1 teaspoon ground nutmeg

1 teaspoon ground cinnamon

1. **To make the eggnog filling:** Chill the bowl of a stand mixer. Fit the mixer with the whisk attachment, then add the heavy cream, eggnog, rum (if using), and 1 tablespoon sugar to the chilled bowl and beat on high speed for 1 to 2 minutes, until the mixture forms stiff peaks. (You can also use a hand mixer.) Cover with plastic wrap and refrigerate for at least 30 minutes.

2. **Meanwhile, make the sugar cookie cups:** Preheat the oven to 350°F (180°C; gas mark 4). Spray a 24-cup mini muffin pan with nonstick cooking spray.

3. In a small bowl, whisk together the 2 tablespoons each sugar and cinnamon.

4. Using clean hands, roll the cookie dough squares into balls and place each ball (about 1 tablespoon) in a prepared muffin cup. Sprinkle each dough ball with some cinnamon sugar.

5. Bake for 8 to 10 minutes, until mostly set but still soft in the middle. Remove from the oven and immediately use the end of a wooden spoon or the back of a measuring teaspoon to press the dough down in the middle to make an indent for the filling. Let cool completely in the pan before running a knife around the edge and removing.

6. Spoon 1 tablespoon of the eggnog mixture into each of the cooled cups and garnish with a dash each of nutmeg and cinnamon.

Notes

- These bites can be made up to 3 days in advance. Store in an airtight container in the refrigerator.

- To make these bites nonalcoholic, leave out the rum.

Index

Bites of Appreciation

If you're reading this, I want to thank YOU! I'm so happy you have *Brilliant Bites* in hand and hope that it brings joy to your home with every bite. Thank you for letting me inspire you as you feed and entertain your loved ones. May the memories you have with each of these bites be fun and oh-so yum!

Thank you to my husband and best friend, Brandon, for your enthusiastic support and encouragement. Doing life with you is so exciting. I can always count on you to advise me and embrace my ambitions. I'm so thankful for your contributions to this book. From the brilliant title to your honest feedback on each recipe to the time you spent crafting each of the incredible cocktail recipes, your commitment to my dreams is one of the many things I love and appreciate about you. Your involvement is so special and something we will cherish forever. I could not do what I do without you! Cheers to a lifetime together. I love you so much!

Lots of love and thanks to our kids, Baker, Bryce, Barrett, and Brookie, for cheering me on and inspiring so much of what I do. Your appreciation for all the fun and yum we have together is what motivates me every day. It's an honor to be your mama. The moments we experience together as a family are something special that we will cherish forever. I hope I inspire you as much as you inspire me and that you always chase your dreams and follow your passions. I'm here for you. I love you more!

Thank you to my mom and dad for your unconditional love and support. I'm so grateful you raised me with such high standards and encouraged me to pursue my passions. The fond memories I have from our home filled with good food and great friends are what inspire me to create these delicious moments. I'm so thankful I inherited your love for cooking and entertaining. It brings so much joy to me and others. Thank you for all that you do for us. I love y'all!

I can't thank Kelsey Foster enough for photographing another masterpiece of a cookbook for me. It came together so beautifully! You are so incredibly talented, and I'm honored to get to work with you. I'm so grateful for the devotion and attention to detail you had for each image in this book. You photograph my recipes so brilliantly, and I truly appreciate the time and energy you put into this. I cherish our friendship and look forward to many more fun photo shoots together. Thank you, thank you!

A huge thank-you to Stephanie Greenwood for working her magic to make each bite look as beautiful as it tastes. You are a master at making food look its best, and I can't thank you enough for pouring so much of your energy and expertise into this cookbook. I have so much trust and respect for what you do, and I'm so grateful you took the lead on logistics to keep us and the recipes on track. I adore you and admire your incredible talent. Cheers to many more delicious moments together!

Thank you so much to Traci Paga for your diligence and dedication in bringing these bites to set looking their best. You are truly talented and never cease to amaze me with the serene way you work to bring recipes to perfection. I'm so thankful for your thoughtfulness and the sense of humor you grace us with when we need it most. It's an honor to get to work with you often!

Thank you to Amanda Mobley for your amazing assistance with styling several of the bites to impress on set. It was such a pleasure working with you! You brought such fun energy and laughter to the kitchen that kept us going strong on some very long days. I appreciate you and look forward to working together again soon!

I'm so thankful to The BakerMama team for all that you did to support and assist me as I created this cookbook and now share it with the world. I truly appreciate your encouragement and excitement every step of the way. I could not do this without your amazing skills and dedication to what we do. We have the dream team, and I'm so grateful each of you are part of it!

Thank you to the entire team, at The Quarto Group for believing in me and giving me the opportunity to bring another amazing cookbook into your kitchens! I'm so grateful to Rage Kindelsperger, my incredible publisher, for her confidence in my creativity and trust that I will create a masterpiece worthy of inspiring people all around the world. I have so much appreciation for Erin Canning, my impressive editor, for the meticulous manner in which she edits my recipes and words throughout each book. I'm so thankful to Laura Drew, my clever creative director, for her diligence in designing such a charming cookbook.

The brilliance of this book would not be possible without each and every one of these very special people in my life. I'm so thankful!

About the Author

MAEGAN BROWN (a.k.a. The BakerMama) is the bestselling cookbook author of *Beautiful Boards* and *Spectacular Spreads*. Her popular food blog, TheBakerMama.com, features hundreds of her tasty recipes and creative meal ideas. She loves to entertain with ease and is passionate about inspiring others to create delicious moments with their loved ones.

Maegan lives in Dallas with her husband and four children. The kitchen is the heart of their home and they love welcoming others into it. You can follow her on Instagram @thebakermama.